THE LIFE AND VISIONS
OF YESHÉ TSOGYAL

T0353006

The Life and Visions of Yeshé Tsogyal

*The Autobiography of the
Great Wisdom Queen*

A TREASURE TEXT DISCOVERED BY
Drimé Kunga

TRANSLATED BY
Chönyi Drolma

FOREWORD BY
Dzongsar Jamyang Khyentse

SNOW LION
BOULDER
2017

Snow Lion
An imprint of Shambhala Publications, Inc.
2129 13th Street
Boulder, Colorado 80302
www.shambhala.com

9 8 7 6 5 4

Printed in the United States of America

Shambhala Publications makes every effort to print on acid-free,
recycled paper.

Snow Lion is distributed worldwide by Penguin Random House, Inc., and
its subsidiaries.

Designed by Gopa & Ted2, Inc.

LIBRARY OF CONGRESS CATALOGING-IN-PUBLICATION DATA

Names: Ye-shes-mtsho-rgyal, active 8th century, author. | Dri-med-kun-dga'.
Title: The Life and Visions of Yeshé Tsogyal: The Autobiography of the
  Great Wisdom Queen / discovered by Drimé Kunga; Translated by Chönyi
  Drolma; Foreword by Dzongsar Jamyang Khyenstse.
Description: First edition. | Boulder: Snow Lion, 2017. | Includes
  bibliographical references and index. | Translated from Tibetan.
Identifiers: LCCN 2016047170 | ISBN 9781611804348 (paperback: alk. paper)
Subjects: LCSH: Ye-shes-mtsho-rgyal, active 8th century. |
  Yoginīs—China—Tibet Autonomous Region—Biography. | BISAC: RELIGION /
  Buddhism / Rituals & Practice. | RELIGION / Buddhism / Sacred Writings. |
  RELIGION / Buddhism / Tibetan.
Classification: LCC BQ998.E757 A3 2017 | DDC 294.3/923092 [B] —dc23
LC record available at https://lccn.loc.gov/2016047170

CONTENTS

FOREWORD

To think of Yeshé Tsogyal only as the consort of Guru Rinpoche is very limited.

Yeshé Tsogyal is actually the voice of Guru Rinpoche. In fact, she *is* Guru Rinpoche in feminine form.

Countless times, Yeshé Tsogyal also leads us to a deeper understanding of the dharma by displaying curiosity and even manifesting as Guru Rinpoche's disciple.

It is no wonder that nearly all the treasure teachings in the Nyingma tradition are in one way or another connected to the Lady Yeshé Tsogyal.

If Guru Rinpoche is the sun, then without any doubt, Yeshé Tsogyal is the sun's rays.

Dzongsar Jamyang Khyentse
June 2016

Message from the Jnanasukha Foundation

This treasure biography of the wisdom dakini Yeshé Tsogyal, a female master of eighth-century Tibet, is a valuable addition to the English-language corpus of her legacy. Its publication is an endeavor of the Jnanasukha Foundation, established in the belief that Yeshé Tsogyal's teachings can lead us to full awakening and a better world.

To make an educated guess, I would be willing to wager that the title, *The Life and Visions of Yeshé Tsogyal: The Autobiography of the Great Wisdom Queen*, is quite irresistible, and that readers might fast-forward to chapter 3, "The Princess Asks Lotus-Born of Oddiyana for Songs of Meditation Instruction." Am I right?

When the crushing circumstances of her position in society are finally resolved, Tsogyal is sealed into a twelve-year retreat. But wait . . . her difficulties are just beginning. She painfully realizes through visionary travels to Oddiyana that although she may be praiseworthy in conventional society, in the context of those dedicated to attaining enlightenment, she is sadly lacking in the basics—genuine faith, diligence, courage, pure vision, and more. Later, even after twelve years of retreat, Tsogyal hears her teacher's assessment: "You still have only a slight understanding of realization and omniscience." How could this be, you might wonder?

It's because the matter of attaining enlightenment is not a soothing pursuit. It's all about cleaning up the mess after the apple cart has been upset. With or without our consent, hardship and difficulties are the way, but whether they become obstacles or not is up to us.

Time and again, Tsogyal is tested by the external and internal until, finally, she has exhausted the potential for distraction. This is precisely the moment she transitions from being a princess, albeit a Dharma princess, to being a dakini, and receives the name Yeshé Tsogyal.

The travails of Tsogyal's life are a precursor to the well-known Milarepa theme: it's not so much the past that counts as it is the navigation of the present in all its complexity. Something very present for me in glimpsing Tsogyal's life through this biography is the amazing mettle of her spirit—something I aspire to but am still in up and down stages. But meanwhile, back on the gradual path, there are other themes more familiar, such as the effect of receiving love and appropriate nurturance to fuel the climb to the mountaintop.

We come to Dharma not just with our questions, but with the way we live our lives. Secret Mantra's spiritual biographies are ostensibly about others, but in point of fact, they are guides into ourselves. This particular biography, a super-intimate, unfiltered look into Tsogyal's struggles and triumphs, helps us remember our wholeness and move into a deeper sense of ourselves. The point is not whether Tsogyal's life actually happened, but that the process of her path is under way within us.

It is a privilege to apply this sacred text to our own lives. May I offer it to you as a homecoming? I encourage you to imagine your own chapter 1, and the following chapters as well, until you can sense your own emergent liberation and enlightened activity to benefit all. Go ahead, walk in the shoes of Yeshé Tsogyal!

And even if this biography projects an unlikely trajectory for us, it can nevertheless shape how we understand ourselves and how we interpret the world. Enlightenment . . . if not now, then later, as Lama Tharchin Rinpoche would say.

To Dzongsar Jamyang Khyentse Rinpoche, receiving your blessings and your praises of Yeshé Tsogyal consecrates this publication as a true source of wisdom for all beings. Thank you for your profound teaching on the significance of Guru Rinpoche and Yeshé Tsogyal in your Foreword.

Most of the dots on the map leading to this publication are invisible. However, to connect a few that I can see, I would like to express my deep gratitude to our exceptional yogini-translator, Chönyi Drolma; our realized commentators Anam Thubten, Chagdud Khadro, Judith Simmer-Brown, Holly Gayley, Khandro Thrinlay Chodon, and Ngawang Zangpo; our diligent editor Ellis Widner; and Shambhala Publications' Nikko Odiseos. Thank you all for carrying the torch.

My own enlightenment teachers have not been my friends. They have always challenged and upset me and brought chaos to my life. May I never separate from them!

LAMA DECHEN YESHE WANGMO was enthroned as a lineage lama in 1992 by Repkong Tsedrup Tharchin Rinpoche. She is the founder of the Jnanasukha Foundation.

SUPPLICATION TO
YESHÉ TSOGYAL

From *The Secret Treasury of Wisdom Dakinis, Dharma Teachings of the Sky Treasury of the Profound Treasures of Namkha Lingpa Rinpoche and Khandro Rinpoche Taré Lhamo*, Tibetan pecha.

Eh ma ho!
In the palace of conceptually transcendent bliss-emptiness,
Samantabhadri, secret Great Mother, you naturally sustain the
    state of bliss.
Please grant your blessings for changeless true bliss to be
    realized and
For the brilliance of wisdom-bliss to be set ablaze!

In the palace of the unborn, unceasing, and changeless,
Secret Yogini, you realized nonarising.
Supplications to you, sambhogakaya Vajra Queen!
Please grant your blessings for the collapse of dualistic mind's
    delusion!

In the palace where beings are tamed through compassion,
Like moons appearing on water, you dance in myriad bodies of
    manifestation.
Supplications at your lotus feet, Yeshé Tsogyal!
Please grant your blessings for the actualization of the
    enlightened intent of the three wisdom bodies!

In all lifetimes, may I and all beings
Be lovingly cared for by the Guru Dakini.
Not entering the wrong paths of incorrect mind and
Never separating from you, may enlightenment be attained as a
    single assembly.

*If you supplicate with these words, with strong faith and devotion,
expressing this prayer as a melodious song of heartfelt longing, you
will actually meet Tsogyal in this life, so what need is there to say
that you will attain liberation?*

Samaya!
Gya Gya Gya!

*To fulfill the request of Gartrul Gelek Nyima, this rendering of
Kharchen Taré Lhamo's symbolic intent was set in writing by
Kapala.*

Sarva Mangalam!

Translated by Lama Dechen Yeshe Wangmo
Hawaii, USA

REFLECTIONS ON
YESHÉ TSOGYAL

INSPIRATIONS FROM YESHÉ TSOGYAL'S NAMTHAR

KHANDRO THRINLAY CHODON

Offering of Praise
Embodiment of the mother of all buddhas—past, present, and
   future.
In the Land of Snows, you appeared in perfection of royalty and
   beauty.
In the midst of wealth and power, you kept the lamp of Dharma
   burning.
With unwavering devotion you won the heart of the Lama
   Lotus-Born.
With all-aspiring diligence you actualized the ultimate view of
   Dzogpachenpo.
It is your unfailing compassion that kept intact
The unfathomable nectar-like treasure of teachings.

It has been an inspiration to have this opportunity to glimpse
into the life of Princess Yeshé Tsogyal. I was fortunate to receive
her empowerment fifteen years ago in the United States from my
beloved uncle, the unmistakable tertön in today's world, His Emi-
nence Namkai Drimed Rinpoche. May these words from an ignorant being like myself bring justice to this biography.

Om Swasti,
I pay homage to the Queen of Bliss—Yeshé Tsogyal!
So that we ignorant beings in this misguided age may drink the
   purity of this truth.

INTRODUCTION AND QUALITIES

Yeshé Tsogyal was no ordinary being. She was an already enlightened dakini, which means she possessed the fully perfected qualities of wisdom and compassion. In essence, she was none other than Arya Tara and Vajrayogini. In appearance, this life story reveals just how her enlightened qualities manifested. Through her life's revelation we too may learn how to journey courageously on the path of ultimate truth within our own flawed lives.

Born in the Land of Snows at Yaru Drak, Yeshé Tsogyal possessed the power and glory of her noble family line. Despite these advantages, she still had to struggle with countless heavy obstacles before becoming the dakini that we know her as today.

It was Yeshé Tsogyal's unmistakable inner qualities and her commitment to developing these that propelled her life toward its true aspiration. Thus, this biography reveals the colors, sounds, and shapes of devotion.

Throughout her life's journey, Yeshé Tsogyal possessed an unfailing determination to free herself from all the trappings of mundane worldly life,

> Completely sacrificed all selfish motives,
> Remained steadfast on the path despite all obstacles, and
> Utilized skillful compassion toward all whom she
> encountered.

Her unwavering dedication to all the above is what enabled her to bring all obstacles into her spiritual path and to actualize the essence of all virtuous qualities in order to benefit countless sentient beings. Such commitment is rare, yet its results are certain.

ASPIRATION AND DEVOTION

Yeshé Tsogyal was an enthralling princess who had all the glamour of royalty and all the material wealth and power that ordinary beings crave. She also possessed captivating beauty and magnetic personal qualities. Yet, these outward attractions were not her aspiration, and they, in fact, became her biggest obstacles. On the path of her spiritual quest, all she wanted was to live in isolation, sustain her body by the elements, and feed on meditative stability.

The eighth century, Guru Rinpoche's era, was not different from today's materialistic world. The same family, social, and political expectations prevailed. Just as is often the case today, in that time, when someone did not comply with these expected norms, they became outcast and objectified. It is very obvious in Yeshé Tsogyal's story that this high-status princess became an object to glorify the family wealth. Her marriage knot had the power to tie national boundaries and improve the social status of its subjects. Therefore, this "poor" princess was under the heaviest pressure to live up to the expectations of her family, the royal officials, and the established political relationships between nations. What appeared to others as such positive life circumstances became for her a huge burden and responsibility that she had to face on the path of Dharma.

No one in the kingdom, not even her own parents, valued her spiritual quest, blinded as they were by greed and selfishness. Yeshé Tsogyal's innate compassion and wisdom were completely ignored.

Yet, despite all these gross obstacles, the princess remained steadfast and devoted to her aspiration, and her strong belief in the power of an open heart became the life force that transformed all situations and any environment. As we read in this biography, even when she is in the "haunted land," the carnivorous beasts became friendly toward her and protected her. The beautiful scented flowers celebrated her with their fragrance and the trees swayed and danced to the melody of chirping birds. When humans failed to understand her, nature supported her and rejoiced in her authenticity. She was unwavering in her devotion, and made every sacrifice. Thus, her deepening inward journey led her to an everlasting happiness that was beyond the false security of material wealth and superficial friends.

Obstacles as Path

Yeshé Tsogyal stood steadfast in her love of the Dharma and spiritual practice. She accepted everything that happened to her and did not blame others or try to hide from her difficulties. Rather, she saw all obstacles on her path as her own and tackled each obstacle with full responsibility and compassionate action. She never blamed anyone but her own karma. She understood and accepted that the current difficult situation was actually a result of her own past deeds, words, and thoughts, even though at this time she could not fully grasp all the interconnections.

> The suffering of one person is not meant for two.
> This princess's past karma
> led the king to reproach me
> and the officials to punish me.
> Though it's unbearable,
> I have to shoulder the burden of my own faults.

This approach to the understanding of suffering is absolutely necessary in these degenerate times, when the art of taking responsibility for our own actions is diminishing. Blame and shame only lead to the promotion of animosity and anger. They are not only unpleasant mental states but are based on a very gross assumption.

Compassionate Action

Yeshé Tsogyal utilized the means of kindness and nonreactivity when working with every obstacle. Even though she was abused physically and verbally by her opponents, she understood their minds and wished them goodness. She did not run away, but tackled each difficulty fearlessly. Cast out by her parents, she offered all her inheritance and willingly lived in the haunted land. She said good-bye, one by one, to all suitors, friends, and attendants, always with words of wisdom and grace, while not hanging on to anything.

Her intrinsic beauty and aspiration were so strong that all obstacles became allies on the journey; she dissolved all into her own beauty. She was like a lotus flower that does not discard the dirt in which it grows, but rather uses that same dirt as the very nutrient that feeds its growth to blossom fully.

In fact, her unwavering commitment, together with the obstacles she faced, pushed Yeshé Tsogyal in the correct spiritual direction to deepen her understanding and apply her compassion. This is the spiritual approach; it courageously welcomes every obstacle to seamlessly transform all meditation and action into pure perception.

REFINING PERCEPTION AND THE FRUIT OF HER ENDURANCE

As spiritual practitioners there is always a time when we are on the verge of giving up. Yeshé Tsogyal was no exception. This time came for her when she felt there was no escape from the bondage of her beautiful female form that everyone objectified. Physically abused, emotionally unheard, and now also spiritually helpless and defeated, she yearned out loud with fervent devotion. As everything was shed, her longing cry melted her guru's unfailing compassion—he came as a white-colored man and his soothing words healed all her wounds.

> Insubstantial mind itself dissolves into space.
> Do not be sad; this is your share of spiritual attainment.
> Meditate on misfortune arising as your ally.

At this point, all her hard work ripened. Her guru confirmed the truth of her path, and he joyfully offered her the pith instructions of the great perfection!

Yeshé Tsogyal was instructed to meditate for twelve years in Samyé Chimpu charnel ground, the place to which she had been magically transported by the Lotus-Born. Here the practice path did not stop for her. Rather, her deepening journey began and she was shown, at increasingly subtle levels, the lack of her devotion and commitment to seeing the true nature of reality.

Our practice is like this—it is an ongoing journey to refine perception and see subtle manifestations of experience as the conditioned and concretized phenomena they are. Like a dancer's movement, the things we accept as real can dissolve, change form, or be experienced in one moment as horrific and in the next, joyful!

How easy it is for us not to go deeper—to stay at our very ordinary, everyday level of perceiving. As spiritual practitioners we have a mere insight and soon get trapped into a feeling of accomplishment. Falling prey to this comfort is a common mistake. We rely on the superficial—like a moth attracted to the flame that causes its death!

It was her guru, this time in the form of a white-colored dakini, who took Yeshé Tsogyal on a science-fiction journey that showed her that her refined perceptions were still deceiving her. First, she was taken to a world where people seemed to struggle and strive to please a king who was unkind and demanding. How many times have we conversed like Yeshé Tsogyal on this topic?

However, it was not a fake king but rather the judgmental and critical mind of Yeshé Tsogyal herself that was revealed. Life as we experience it is just an apparition. Only by giving up our fixated view can we see something different. By journeying in these sometimes weird and terrifying lands, Yeshé Tsogyal got to see, again and again, how experiences are hallucinations. She saw that when one lacks faith, this results in a superficial understanding. With each step on her journey, Yeshé Tsogyal saw the mistake of impoverished faith. Increasingly, she began to trust herself enough to believe and act from the ever-present and spacious mind, from which abundant courage, wisdom, and compassion unceasingly radiate.

At the end of her heavenly tour, all of Yeshé Tsogyal's subtle doubts, expectations, and perceptions were purified. The Awareness Holder of Spontaneous Ever-presence unveiled himself in dark-blue color with a wrathful gaze. He then conferred upon her the empowerment of the fourfold joy of great bliss! She was now a perfect recipient of the awareness lineage. At this point, with her guru, she courageously cleared all her doubts through piercingly profound questions.

At every point, her guru has been there, appearing in different forms to challenge, clarify, and even push her toward a deepening trust. As practitioners we have little insight and such a huge, stagnant ego about our accomplishments. It is a sober moment in the Yeshé Tsogyal story when, practicing the highest instruction, our heroine is invited to keep refining her boundless compassion. Even in her highly realized state, Yeshé Tsogyal wanted to take the comfortable route to help beings in the pure lands. However, her wrathful master cut her ego and gave her an even harder task— to go to hell and release Shanti, the evil official who had always blocked her path! She did so, and this was the act of nondual service that purified her most subtle obscuration and empowered her for recognition as the courageous dakini, enabling the bestowing of the auspicious name Yeshé Tsogyal.

At this point, the Lotus-Born acknowledged that his own refined qualities came from her wisdom. Masculine and feminine, guru and student, are playful forms in the display of dreamlike appearances.

Eh ma ho!
Thanks to our precious dakini, Yeshé Tsogyal!
Your life story holds all truth and is still relevant to us
    impoverished spiritual students.
You persevered to keep the lamp burning for our degenerate
    times.
You kept the essence of the pith instructions and hid them as
    treasures in the elements, to be revealed by realized tertöns.
May you appear again and again to inspire and guide all
    complicated beings in this chaotic world!

KHANDRO THRINLAY CHODON'S family is a holder of the Drukpa Kargyud lineage. She married the Ninth Shabdrung, Ngawang Jigme, head of the Drukpa lineage of Bhutan, in 1998 and participated in the establishment of several of his monasteries prior to his death in 2003. Her spiritual master recognized Khandro-la's capacity to manifest Dharma activities and gave the name "Khachodling" to her vision of Dharma and humanitarian projects. This has become her life's work of spiritual training and activity.

Our Incalculable Debt to Yeshé Tsogyal

Anam Thubten Rinpoche

Ancient Tibet lies between the great civilizations of India and China, whose rich cultures have extended great influence on their neighbors. The boundaries among Asiatic nations have fluctuated dramatically over time. At certain periods in history, Tibet had powerful empires ruling vast lands and great populations that rivaled those of other Asiatic powers.

In the beginning, Tibet's main spirituality was indigenous shamanism based mainly on oral tradition. In the seventh century, King Songtsen Gampo married a Chinese princess and sent his minister, Thönmi Sambhota, to India to study languages and Buddhism in order to develop a written language for Tibet. Songsten Gampo built temples and had texts translated from Sanskrit into Tibetan. During his lifetime, Buddhism in Tibet was still quite new and his people didn't completely embrace it.

Buddhism began taking deeper root and became a complete tradition in Tibet during the long reign of King Trisong Detsen in the eighth century. He invited yogis and scholars from India and other countries to translate sutras, tantras, and shastras into Tibetan, including the Buddhist canon. He built Samyé Monastery as the first true Buddhist learning center in his country. Shantarakshita established the monastic order by ordaining Tibetans as monks during that time. Later, the great Mahasiddha Padmasambhava brought tantric Buddhism and Dzogchen teachings and created a yogic order. Many Tibetans became enlightened through his teachings, and some of his famous students are known as the twenty-five disciples. This was a golden age for Tibet in every respect, both spiritually and politically. Historical texts often describe Shantarakshita, Guru Padmasambhava, and King Trisong Detsen as the three individuals responsible for establishing the complete Buddhist tradition in Tibet.

But there is another individual who is equally important in performing such tasks and that is the dakini Yeshé Tsogyal. She was born into a noble family and later became a great yogini and the closest disciple of Guru Padmasambhava. Padmasambhava gave many profound tantric and Dzogchen teachings because she requested them. She taught and maintained Padmasambhava's lineage. We are indebted to her, because if not for her, we wouldn't be able to enjoy these priceless teachings in Tibetan Buddhism, especially of the Nyingma lineage. Someone like me who was born into the Nyingma tradition and benefited tremendously from its teachings feels a strong affinity with and gratitude toward her.

I'm so excited to see that Yeshé Tsogyal's biography, revealed by Tertön Drimé Kunga, has been translated into English. This will be of benefit to many, giving a window into her enlightened life that can be a powerful source of inspiration and devotion. This book illustrates more than her exterior life; it also elucidates her supreme secret life of awakening, her journey into the unconditioned or nirvana. It's called "supremely secret" because this aspect of life cannot be easily seen by the outside world. Usually, in the Tibetan tradition, writings on the life of saints, mystics, and mahasiddhas that can be seen are called "outer" biography. Many of the events that take place in the secret biography of masters are to be regarded as parts of a transcendental journey unfolding in their "inner" world of spiritual awakening. Most of Yeshé Tsogyal's life story is found in revelatory writings, such as those attributed to Taksham Dorjé. She is mentioned in the ancient historical record *The Testament of Ba* (*Sba bzhed*), which is the most reliable text on the establishment of Buddhism in Tibet during King Trisong Detsen's reign. The author was a member of the king's court.

This is an inspiring sacred text from the spiritual point of view.

It contains beautifully written prose with the power to move our hearts. It describes Yeshé Tsogyal as an authentic human being, who went through successive trials and tribulations. It shows that, in the beginning, she confronted many challenges in her determination to cultivate *bodhicitta*, the burning desire to be enlightened for the sake of all living beings. She was objectified and mistreated by others, even her loved ones. What hardship she had to go through! It's something we can relate to quite easily. Her humanness can be a bridge between ourselves and enlightenment, which appears to be beyond our comprehension. On the one hand, she is enlightened and exalted; on the other hand, she is completely human and was not spared life's hardships. This gives us, who feel so ordinary, an aspiration for inner liberation. She is a true bodhisattva who never runs away for the sake of ordinary solace, and she invites the most unfavorable circumstances when it is necessary for her inner awakening.

The text gives us a clear image of her being a true *tantrika* who undertook the path of devotion. Devotion is considered one of the main methods in tantric Buddhism. It leads one to total surrender, which leads to letting go of obsessive grasping to oneself, as well as to dualistic concepts. In a sense, devotion can be regarded as an ecstatic, heart-oriented path that's dynamic and amazingly transformative. We can experience true surrender through devotion toward various objects, such as a deity, a buddha, or a guru. Cultivating devotion toward a guru might be a unique practice of the Vajrayana as far as Buddhism is concerned. Such practice can be quite powerful, especially when the guru is an embodiment of love and wisdom. One of the high points in her life is her relationship with Guru Padmasambhava, who embraced her with unconditional love. One can say that she's fortunate to have met with not just any guru, but Padmasambhava, who is considered by Tibetan Buddhists to be the second Buddha, the ocean of all the enlightened qualities. Other guru-disciple relationships, such as those between Tilopa and Naropa and between Marpa and Milarepa, are testimony to how powerful this path can be.

This biography shows not only that Yeshé Tsogyal is courageous and full of egoless devotion to her path and to her guru, but also that she is a wisdom holder at the highest level. As a matter of fact, the first part of her name is the word "*yeshé*," which means "primordial wisdom." This is the same as the term "*sahaja jina*" in the Vajrayana tradition, which is the inborn wisdom that knows the deepest truth of everything, including one's true nature. Such insight goes beyond intellect or conceptual knowledge. She is someone with the deepest insight into emptiness who has the richness of love and compassion. This is why she became an extraordinary master with the ability to teach the most profound Dharma and awaken others in her lifetime. She is regarded as one of the main masters of the Dzogchen lineage.

Yeshé Tsogyal is revered as an enlightened being in a human body, inseparable from Buddha Samantabhadri and Vajravarahi. In the Nyingma lineage, we regard her as one of the main lineage masters. We practice her *sadhana*, where she is portrayed in the form of a divine tantric goddess or a dakini. One example of this is a sadhana revealed by Jigme Lingpa in which she appears in the form of Vajrayogini. In the past, this particular sadhana was practiced by almost all the Nyingma monasteries.

In the end, you can regard both Padmasambhava and Yeshé Tsogyal as founding masters of the Nyingma lineage. Even today, her teachings are constantly influencing the minds and hearts of many. Her teachings mainly came down through the visionary revelations of various tertöns.

There could have been Tibetan yoginis prior to her, yet it's fair to say that Yeshé Tsogyal is the first notable Tibetan woman who became a great master from practicing Buddhism. This confirms that she is an important historical figure, like some of those spiritual icons who will remain in our collective memory for many generations. After her, there were many female mystics, saints, and mahasiddhas in Tibetan Buddhism, such as Machik Labdrön. In general, the Nyingma tradition has produced a great number of revered female masters, from the past to the present. It's also inspiring to see that many excellent women Dharma teachers are emerging in both the East and the West in the present time.

I'm so thankful to Lama Yeshe Wangmo for creating this biography in English. She has been a good friend of mine for many years. She is a wonderful Western Dharma teacher who has completed the traditional three-year retreat twice, is a master of sacred rituals, and is very learned in the doctrine. Above all, she is someone who embodies inner wisdom and lives the Dharma. She has been working tirelessly to share the wisdom of Yeshé Tsogyal for many years. Lama Wangmo has also been helping the nunnery at Tsogyal Latso in Tibet, the birthplace of Yeshé Tsogyal. Recently, Lama Wangmo built a beautiful temple, which is a big blessing to the nuns. I'm thankful to her for all the good things she's doing in this world. Many thanks to the translator, Chönyi Drolma, and to Shambhala Publications for collaborating in this endeavor.

ANAM THUBTEN RINPOCHE is the founder and spiritual adviser of the Dharmata Foundation. He is the author of *Embracing Each Moment* (Shambhala, 2016), *No Self, No Problem: Awakening to Our True Nature* (Shambhala, 2013), and *The Magic of Awareness* (Shambhala, 2012).

Yeshé Tsogyal, the Guiding Light

Chagdud Khadro

The writings of Dakini Yeshé Tsogyal shine almost unbearable brilliance into the dark and clouded recesses of my mind. Flaws, doubts, inadequacies, rationalizations, procrastinations, and hypocrisies find undeniable exposure. It is never comfortable.

Yet, her voice, sweet and melodious across the centuries, beckons and gives confidence. Her stories, confided with such intimacy, provide guidance as I wend my way through outer and inner spiritual obstacles. Her presence, always accessible if I remember and request it, is ever luminous and softens the conflicted emotions and confusion that arise within me during these chaotic, degenerate times.

Yeshé Tsogyal, again and again, asked spiritual questions of the Lotus-Born Guru Rinpoche on behalf of us all. These were amazing questions posed in an orderly sequence that evoke clear and full responses which delineate the path to complete liberation and enlightenment. How can we not be grateful, not only for the teachings themselves, but also for the example of a consummate union of the guru-disciple relationship?

Here in my center in southern Brazil, we have two statues and several paintings of Yeshé Tsogyal. These have power because they have been created by skilled artists and consecrated by realized rinpoches, but Yeshé Tsogyal eludes captivity in art. It is only through our prayers and meditation that her resplendent beauty reveals itself. She embodies radiant bliss and wisdom beyond ordinary perception.

Chagdud Tulku Rinpoche's mother, Delog Dawa Drolma, in her journey in realms beyond death, encountered Dakini Yeshé Tsogyal in Guru Rinpoche's palace on the Copper-Colored Mountain of Glory. After singing a song of aspiration, Yeshé Tsogyal accompanied Dawa Drolma's departure for one hundred paces, saying, "Other than the small distance that I have come today, I actually never go anywhere." How wonderful to stay in one place yet to be everywhere!

As I read *The Supreme Secret Biography of Yeshé Tsogyal, Chief Dakini* on my computer screen, several times I found my hands spontaneously placed in the gesture of prayer. I offer homage not only to Dakini Yeshé Tsogyal and the Lotus-Born Guru Rinpoche but also to the inspired translator, Chönyi Drolma, and the sponsor, Lama Dechen Yeshe Wangmo, of the Jnanasukha Foundation. May their aspirations for this precious text be fulfilled and may all with fortunate connection be blessed by it, for their benefit and for the benefit of all beings.

CHAGDUD KHADRO is the spiritual director of Chagdud Gonpa Brasil. She married Chagdud Tulku Rinpoche in 1979 and was enthroned as a lama by him in 1997. Chagdud Khadro collaborated with Rinpoche for his autobiography *Lord of the Dance* (Padma Publishing, 1992) and compiled commentaries of his teachings on the Düdjom Tersar Ngöndro, Longsal Nyingpo Phowa, and the concise Red Tara practice of Apang Tertön.

Mother of the Victorious Ones

Acharya Judith Simmer-Brown

In 1959, my root guru, Vidyadhara Chögyam Trungpa Rinpoche, narrowly escaped with his life in the midst of fleeing Tibet with a large group of devotees. He briefly found refuge in the hidden land of Pema Kö, and there in a natural rock cave, he spontaneously sang a long song of thanksgiving to Yeshé Tsogyal with a repeating refrain:

> Mother of all the victorious ones, so very kind Ama Tsogyal,
> Refuge for this life and on, very kind mother, I miss you.
> This little child, thinking of Ama, simply can't bear it at all—
> Ama, a la la, please truly show me a clear sign of your
>   blessings.*

This haunting and penetrating song speaks of Yeshé Tsogyal as Ama, the Mother of the Victorious Ones, the buddhas. This image of mother captures multiple aspects of Yeshé Tsogyal's life and its importance for all Tibetan Buddhist practitioners. She provides ancestral and spiritual lineage, wisdom realization, and protection for all who faithfully follow the path.

When Trungpa Rinpoche supplicated Yeshé Tsogyal, he tapped into the powerful current of blessings that flows through

---

* Nalanda Translation Committee, "Sunshine for a Pauper: A Spontaneous Song of Supplication to the Mother-Lineage Guru of the Great Secret," 2008. http://nalandatranslation.org/offerings/translations-and-commentaries/the-wisdom-of-the-feminine/.

her ancestral and spiritual lineages. Yeshé Tsogyal is called "Mother of the Victorious Ones" to signify that symbolically she is an emanation of Prajnaparamita herself, the realization that all phenomena are unborn, unproduced, and without end. This emblematic teaching is the essence of all Buddhism; realization of this nondual truth is said to completely transform the practitioner's experience and journey, and to activate the inherent buddhahood within. Realization of emptiness is called the "ultimate *shunyata* protection" in Mahayana Buddhism, because when the true nature of phenomena is known, conventional dangers and worries are seen as dreamlike apparitions, and skillful determinations of the path ahead become clear.

But more than this, Rinpoche tied himself to the guru lineages of Guru Rinpoche and the Nyingma, to the deepest realizations of Tibet's spiritual teachings from the *terma* lineages, to the sacred land of Tibet itself, and to the intrepid faithfulness of the Tibetan people in the face of adversity and tribulation. Yeshé Tsogyal represents all of these aspects, as she was likely the very first Tibetan to attain enlightenment, and as a devoted disciple of Guru Rinpoche, she became the progenitor of the entire tradition of realization of the yogic practices of Tibet. She is the most famous dakini, a powerful female emblem of the ultimate realization joining the sacredness of the body, both female and male; the profound meeting point of body and mind in meditation; the visionary realm of ritual practice; and the empty, spacious qualities of mind itself.* Dakinis became symbols of realization in Tibetan tantra and, as visionary beings, preside over the gates of wisdom for practitioners to come. Yeshé Tsogyal is universally recognized as Queen of the Dakinis.

Evidence that Yeshé Tsogyal was a historical woman, a principal disciple of Guru Rinpoche, living from 757–817 C.E., grounds the rich lore of her life example for contemporary women

---

* Judith Simmer-Brown, *Dakini's Warm Breath: The Feminine Principle in Tibetan Buddhism* (Boston: Shambhala, 2001).

practitioners.* Accounts of her life detail the specific obstacles she faced as a woman—manipulated by parents with marital plans to cement political alliances, vied over by royal suitors because of her noble line, assailed by outlaws on retreat, heckled by would-be patrons, and tested by teachers regarding her intentions and depth of realization. Throughout her journey, she herself questions her aptitude even while remaining true to her practice and her guru's instructions. Her deep faith and stamina in the practice provide tremendous inspiration for practitioners in the intervening centuries, as her enlightenment was not granted by miraculous means. She did it the hard way; she earned it.

As Guru Rinpoche's closest disciple, she is said to be transcriber for his treasure teachings, using a lock of her own hair to calligraph in the secret dakini code, decipherable only to the most worthy of tertöns. These treasure texts, rediscovered at auspicious times throughout Tibetan history, prove their profundity by their skillful addressing of changing times, demonstrating the "fresh warm breath" of authentic teachings. This pivotal role has engraved Yeshé Tsogyal into the hearts of Tibetans as the enduring mother of realization. At her death, Yeshé Tsogyal vows that she will continuously respond to supplications for protection, blessing, and realization into the future, establishing her as an enduring, timeless figure in the Tibetan imagination. There have been myriad emanations of her throughout Tibetan history, and relics of hair, dakini script, articles of clothing, and ritual implements have been discovered across a

* While there is no clear historical evidence of a Tibetan queen named Yeshé Tsogyal, her early appearance in Tibetan accounts (as early as the twelfth century) suggest Yeshé Tsogyal may well have been a queen whose life became the basis of much of the tantric lore that follows her. Janet Gyatso, "A Partial Genealogy of the Lifestory of Ye she's mtsho rgyal." *Journal of the International Association of Tibetan Studies*, no. 2 (August 2006). These dates come from Keith Dowman, trans., *Sky Dancer: The Secret Life and Songs of the Lady Yeshe Tsogyel* (London: Routledge & Kegan Paul, 1984), 343–44. It is famously difficult to date the lives of the siddhas, especially when they are women. Rita Gross credits this to what she calls "quadruple androcentrism." See *Buddhism After Patriarchy* (Albany: SUNY Press, 1992), 18.

broad landscape. To this day, she appears in dreams and visions, offering encouragement, advice, and prophecy to those who supplicate her. From this perspective, Yeshé Tsogyal adds lineage authority to her enduring presence for Tibetan Buddhist practitioners.

In this context, the publication of a new biography of Yeshé Tsogyal, revealed by Drimé Kunga, is a joyous occasion. Tracing the journey of the Queen of Dakinis, the biography has all the classic elements of a *namthar*, from her miraculous birth, her contested betrothal, and her spiritual journey fraught with obstacles and their resolution, transmissions and teachings, and their realization.

There are three distinctive elements in this biography that will provide fresh perspective about the life of Yeshé Tsogyal. First, there is no mention of the Tibetan emperor Trisong Detsen, often listed as her husband, in the *Secret Biography*. The account of her contested betrothal proceeds in tremendous detail, with arguments presented by her family and various members of the court, with Yeshé Tsogyal's rejoinder, insisting that she only wished a life of practice and retreat. The agonizing betrothal drama encompasses forty percent of the entire biography, with endless scenes of abduction, beatings, unsuccessful seductions, the princess's bribery of her entire retinue with her dowry, and fruitless escapes. In a final desperate scene, the princess prays for a protector who could provide her sanctuary, and a white-colored man with his hair knotted around a crystal, holding a turquoise vase, appears to her and praises her faith and commitment. Declaring himself to be Guru Rinpoche, he offers to accompany her, and presents her with a jeweled ring, asking her to hold him doubtlessly on the crown of her head, promising that the court and kingdom will no longer be able to see her. Together they fly to a sacred charnel ground called Samyé Chimpu, a powerful place for tantric practice. To protect the frustrated royals from further violence, Guru Rinpoche furnishes two cloned princesses to substitute for Tsogyal, who delight their respective kingdoms.

The second distinctive contribution to Yeshé Tsogyal's biography comes in the form of a detailed visionary journey to Oddiyana during the twelve years of her solitary retreat in Samyé Chimpu charnel ground. This journey exposes her to kingdoms and beings both virtuous and despicable. She is tested on her commitments, her prudery and squeamishness, and her courage, and given specific tasks to fulfill and practices to complete. One of the most striking accounts evokes the famous jataka tale from the Buddha's previous life, in which the princess offers herself as food for a tigress and her eighteen cubs that are starving, dehydrated, and close to death. As the princess hacks her own body to pieces as an offering, the tigress smiles in admiration and heals her wounds, nursing her back to health in gratitude. This powerful act of compassion accelerates Tsogyal's spiritual progress and emboldens her in facing the many challenges in Oddiyana.

Third, at the point when Yeshé Tsogyal is about to become enlightened, she is challenged by a wrathful apparition, who asks if she is actually able to help anyone. He sends her to the hell realms to test her realization, and suggests that she especially liberate an evil official named Shanti, who had posed many obstacles in her path. The biography details her descent through the hell realms, her witnessing of the tortures of many beings, her practice for beings in the Hell of Endless Torment, and her liberation of those beings, including Shanti. This final act accomplishes her enlightenment, earns her the name Victorious Ocean of Wisdom, and brings the following praises from Guru Rinpoche:

You are a fully qualified dakini
And the mother who gives life
to all triumphant buddhas.
Yours is the great force of all buddhas,
As the motherly loving protector
Of all beings of the six realms.

> My own qualities as Lotus-Born
> Don't come from me—
> They come from you.*

In these words, this biography seals her legacy as Mother of the Victorious Ones.

Why would Drimé Kunga's biography emphasize new themes and events of Yeshé Tsogyal's life? The answer may be found in the terma's responsiveness to the challenge of our times, and three recurrent themes can be discovered in the text. The first theme is faith. Again and again, Tsogyal's faith is challenged by adversity, from the protracted struggle to remain unmarried through her visionary spiritual journey. The first teaching that Guru Rinpoche gives her is how to see adversity as the path, and this is when she is able to fully enter retreat. When she remains steady, she is praised for the strength of her faith.

The second theme is courage. The princess faces terrifying obstacles, ranging from family disinheritance to physical torture and imprisonment, as well as threats from terrifying demons and wrathful heroes and dakinis. Her mentors chide her for her fear and intimidation, and eventually she is able to directly question the bizarre visions that she endures. In order to overcome the worst of these nightmarish visions, she is given a subtle-body yogic practice to clear her channels and purify her personal karma. Supported by the tigress's encouragement, she becomes fearless in the face of threats.

The third theme that pervades the *Secret Biography* is kindness. Throughout the princess's travails, she is able to sustain her empathy for beings and to return kindness for the cruelty and savagery she encounters. This is most clear in her encounters in the hell realms, where her practice for the liberation of her previous enemy brought her final enlightenment. For this mastery, Guru Rinpoche promises that she will be ever responsive to the entreaties of practitioners, and that her "nondual compassion will transform

---

* *The Supreme Secret Biography of Yeshé Tsogyal, Chief Dakini*, pp. 184–85.

into anything at all."* In this degenerate age of aggression and fear, the *Secret Biography* promises us that the Mother of the Victorious Ones is always available with her enduring faith, her quiet courage, and her unfailing compassion.

———————

ACHARYA JUDITH SIMMER-BROWN, PHD, is a senior Dharma teacher in the Shambhala lineage of Chögyam Trungpa and Sakyong Mipham, and Distinguished Professor of Contemplative and Religious Studies at Naropa University. She is the author of *Dakini's Warm Breath: The Feminine Principle in Tibetan Buddhism* (Shambhala, 2002) and *Meditation and the Classroom: Contemplative Pedagogy for Religious Studies* (SUNY Press, 2011).

* *The Supreme Secret Biography of Yeshé Tsogyal, Chief Dakini,* p. 185.

In the Company of
Angels and Saints

Ngawang Zangpo

The word "buddha" in Tibetan—*sangyé*—is not problematic to
Tibetan ears. That is to say, it is not heard as a gender-specific term.
Thousands upon thousands of girls are given that name at birth
(just as boys are); it is far more common than the gender-exclusive
name "Jesus" in Hispanic cultures. Calling an infant girl Sangyé—
Buddha—is completely unremarkable.

Yes, there is only one "Buddha" in our era, but in his wake millions of buddhas, female and male, have attained an enlightenment
equally full and complete. It is, after all, our ever-present nature:
even before we were born, we were born this way. Each of us can
realize our own enlightened nature and become the buddha we
already are.

I mention this as a preamble to what in Tibetan is an obvious
statement, but one that might seem provocative to our ears: Yeshé
Tsogyal is a buddha. I think it's important to say it like that, at least
once. Below, I sometimes use a gender-neutral term not without
complications—*saint*—because we all reflexively know sainthood
to be open to one and all.

Yeshé Tsogyal is often referred to as a "dakini," a Sanskrit word
that is also not gender specific in its Tibetan version—*khandro*. In
this autobiography, we find the term defined as an individual who
freely moves (*'gro*) in the unlimited pure space (*mkha'*) of the pan-
oramic wakefulness that arose of itself and is ours from the start.

It might sound transgressive to say this in non-Buddhist languages, but all enlightened beings are *khandro*. Our word that

approximates *khandro* is "angel" (*angelos* in Greek; *malak* in Hebrew; both meaning "messenger"). In biblical scripture, angels are exclusively adult males; only three are named—Michael, Gabriel, and Lucifer. Common imagination now seems to confine angels either to presexual children of either gender or to idealized, unlikely-to-be-attained female objects of desire. What is positive about the word "angel" is that many people sense them anywhere and everywhere, which is how we Buddhists understand our angels and saints.

Language is a minefield, but so are our minds.

This autobiography of Yeshé Tsogyal is quite different from the one translated into English a number of times (as *Lady of the Lotus-Born*, for example). Outside Buddhism's common founda-tion (Hinayana), accounts of the deeds of enlightened beings are not meant primarily as backward-looking documents, what we consider history. The lives of saints are meant to lead us forward: their purpose is to spur us to unearth and awaken our inner Yeshé Tsogyal. This was her intention in writing autobiographies, the intention of the masters who revealed this work from her concealed treasures, the intention of the publishers of the original Tibetan edition and of this modern translation, and the intention of Lama Yeshe Wangmo of the Jnanasukha Foundation and the translator they sponsored, Chönyi Drolma. So many bodies, only one mind.

How can you begin to awaken your inner Yeshé Tsogyal? First, one must have faith in the cornerstone of all Buddhists' faith: in your own enlightened nature, unchanged since before the dawn of time. Then, you must find an enlightened master, a saint. To do so, you will likely have to leave the security of your home and even your homeland. You can't plan for anything beyond this, any more than you can choose when and where and how and with whom you fall in love. But you must prioritize your search.

Yeshé Tsogyal, as with any buddha before her, had to turn entirely away from the narrative that greeted her at birth. She found class identity, racial identity, national identity, gender identity, the fact that one was privileged or disadvantaged, and so on, to all be mundane ties that were worse than useless. Chains of lead and chains of gold bind us equally. Most women learn the truth before men: the round of rebirth, our human rat race, is rotten at its core.

Yeshé Tsogyal had to encounter a fully qualified master. This was no easy task. She found her guru and spent twelve years in retreat, only to be informed at its conclusion that she had collected a wealth of experiences without it amounting to realization. She was so crestfallen she fainted. But she had given everything, body and soul, to her spiritual path; she mustered the courage to take the final decisive steps to enlightenment. So it is that we now bow our heads, holding nothing back, at her feet. She is our guru, our lama, our mother, our father, our sister, our brother, our friend, our lover, our everything, ourselves.

My words here are numbered. I will spend just a few to curse the darkness of the past ten thousand years: the second-class status of the lowborn, as Yeshé Tsogyal refers to herself, using the common Tibetan term/slur for a "wombed human." She uses it as a formulaic token of her sincere humility, an essential qualification for spiritual apprenticeship. Guru Rinpoche mirrors it back. It's not personal. In fact, as grating as the term "lowborn" is to our sensibilities, it accurately reflects women's standing everywhere on this sorry planet. We live in the hope that our past will not jinx our future. Darkness visits this world; women get more than their fair share of it and to a degree we men can scarcely imagine. But there can be light.

The first time I was conscious of meeting a living incarnation of Yeshé Tsogyal was in 1973. I would sometimes run into a Tibetan woman on the street, and we would pause a moment to chat. She worked as a housekeeper to help support her three young children. She would laugh and tell stories of her acclimatizing to the comical aspects of Canadian life. Years later, after her retirement, she ceased pretending to be an ordinary individual and began to teach. She is a living buddha, a saint, an embodied, awakened angel called Jetsun Kushok Rinpoche. My daughter is named after another wonderful saint, Kunzang Wangmo, whom you can meet in a film by Jody Kemmerer called *Sky Dancer* (www.skydancermovie.com).

The female buddha I've been closest to, Khandro Tsering Chödrön, was born in the same tiny village as Kalu Rinpoche. Over some years, I visited her in the single, small room she inhabited alone in Sikkim. She would talk, sing mantras, and show me photo albums of herself in different kinds of dress, including Indian saris and Western pants. She found in anything a reason to laugh. "Everyone calls me *khandro*" (literally, "one who moves through the sky"), she complained. "What am I, some sort of bird?" she would say, with yet another infectious giggle. When the Dalai Lama gave the Kalachakra empowerment to thousands in Sikkim, he had her sit on the stage with him. When she passed away, her body demonstrated miraculous signs that might seem like unverifiable tales from an inaccessible land, except that they occurred in 2011 near Montpelier, France. That is where Chönyi Drolma and I last visited her, a short time before her death. Khandro Tsering Chödrön's picture will sit facing me on my desk along with that of Kalu Rinpoche until I die. You can use vacation time to visit a living buddha, including a female saint.

Don't believe what some skeptics claim, that there are few female buddhas, now or ever. When a rational materialist meets a saint, he questions whether she's a saint at all, especially if she has no titles, no prestige, no institutions, no written histories, no public following, no big ambitions, and no vanity projects. But don't be fooled: many fully empowered and realized incarnations of Yeshé Tsogyal live hidden among us in plain sight. They found their Guru Rinpoche, and followed the teachings to enlightenment. Believe.

NGAWANG ZANGPO is a translator with the Tsadra Foundation. His books include *The Complete Nyingma Tradition from Sutra to Tantra, Books 1 to 10: Foundations of the Buddhist Path* (Snow Lion, 2014); *The Treasury of Knowledge, Books 2, 3, and 4: Buddhism's Journey to Tibet* (Snow Lion, 2010); and *Guru Rinpoche: His Life and Times* (Snow Lion, 2002).

Yeshé Tsogyal as Female Exemplar

Holly Gayley

Yeshé Tsogyal has been hailed as the "foremost female figure" in the Nyingma tradition, an "outstanding female religious master" of Tibet's imperial period, the "enlightened consort" of Padmasambhava, and the "pre-eminent female exemplar" for Tibetan women.[*] Though we know little about her as a historical person, Yeshé Tsogyal appears widely in Buddhist ritual, art, and literature as the Tibetan consort of the eighth-century Indian tantric master Padmasambhava, a frequent visionary guide for Buddhist masters, an ongoing centerpiece for devotion in tantric liturgies, and an important antecedent for Tibetan women who have been identified as her emanations.[†] New sources for Yeshé Tsogyal's life have recently come to light, including the version by Drimé Kunga (fourteenth century) translated in this book, which was initially located in 1996 by Janet Gyatso and later published in 2008 by Khenpo Palden Sherab and Sky Dancer Press.[‡] Through this source, we get a glimpse into the evolution of her life story, revealed some three hundred years prior to the version by Taksham Nuden Dorjé (seventeenth century), known to English readers through

---

[*] These characterizations come from, in order, Gyatso 2006, Uebach 2005, Gross 1987, and again Gyatso 2006.

[†] On liturgies with a focus on Yeshé Tsogyal, see Klein 1994.

[‡] The Tibetan is available as an e-book at www.skydancerpress.com/ebooks/tsogyalnamthar.pdf.

the following published translations: *Mother of Knowledge* (1983), *Sky Dancer* (1996), and *Lady of the Lotus-Born* (1999).*

Unlike the chronological narrative of Yeshé Tsogyal's life by Taksham, Drimé Kunga focuses on a key set of dramatic episodes in her spiritual quest. A lengthy account is given of the youthful princess resisting her parents' wishes for her to marry, with a different ending than Taksham provides. Instead of Yeshé Tsogyal becoming one of the queens of the Tibetan emperor Trisong Detsen, in Drimé Kunga's rendering she is exiled for her disobedience.† When one of her princely suitors later kidnaps the exiled princess, Padmasambhava arrives just in time to rescue her and whisk her away to the meditation hermitage at Samyé Chimpu. Following that, the rest of the work consists mainly of extended visionary sequences and esoteric instructions from Padmasambhava. Accordingly, the attention shifts from Yeshé Tsogyal's outer beauty and desirability to suitors toward her development of inner qualities and realization. The choice to privilege these elements over the flow of her outer activities has much to do with the work's claim in its title to be a "secret biography."‡ As a subgenre, this refers to a story of "complete liberation" (*rnam thar*), usually the biography of a Buddhist master, that proposes to be "secret" (*gsang ba*) to the extent that it emphasizes visionary experience.

Due to its esoteric nature and a number of gruesome scenes that take place in pure lands and hell realms alike, let me suggest an allegorical reading of this work as a depiction of the tantric journey in gendered terms.§ Given her exile after refusing to marry, in

---

* See respectively Tarthang Tulku 1983, Dowman 1996, and Padmakara Translation Group 1999.

† Gyatso 2006 discusses differences between these two versions of Yeshé Tsogyal's life story at length.

‡ See Gyatso 1998: 6–8 on the categories of outer, inner, and secret in Tibetan autobiography. Drimé Kunga's version of her life presumes to be narrated by Yeshé Tsogyal herself, but the first person voice comes to the fore mainly in its framing.

§ An allegorical reading is supported by the subtitle of the work, "the exceptional inner meaning of symbols" (*thun min nang gi brda don*).

Drimé Kunga's rendering of her life, Yeshé Tsogyal begins alone on her quest for spiritual perfection. Along the way, she finds herself in a diverse array of settings—haunted jungles, stark retreat caves, bejeweled palaces in pure lands, and the ravages of hell—each of which elicit in her certain lessons and spiritual qualities. Although Padmasambhava arrives just in time to rescue her, shortly thereafter he leaves Yeshé Tsogyal to practice in solitary retreat for twelve years. Later, a dakini appears to guide her on a visionary journey through pure lands, represented as various kingdoms within the land of Oddiyana, but likewise at a certain point leaves her to her own devices. While getting help along the way, it is up to Yeshé Tsogyal herself to find the appropriate gateway into the tantric teachings and prove herself worthy to enter.

Allegorically, the challenges she confronts could be read as tests of her worthiness to receive tantric initiation and further teachings. Each time, she proves herself, not through devotion as one might expect but through her immense compassion. This is first apparent when Yeshé Tsogyal transforms the haunted jungle of her exile into an oasis with wild animals frolicking around her, tamed by her beneficent presence. Compassion comes to the fore again on her visionary journey to Oddiyana, in which the monarchs of each dazzling kingdom represent the guru principle and their subjects show devotion through extreme acts of self-abnegation. Their dedication shames Yeshé Tsogyal, who considers her own faith to be fickle by comparison. Some of their acts are disturbing, as when a crowd ingests poison at the command of their king, a scene all too reminiscent of Jonestown for the contemporary reader. Notably, Yeshé Tsogyal rejects such austerities and misses, again and again, the opportunity for instantaneous enlightenment. Later, it is revealed that the residents of these realms are actually celestial male and female deities, which she cannot recognize due to impure perception. Thus, in an allegorical reading, the quick path of such extreme devotion is not for humans. It is after all a dangerous pursuit, signaled by pervasive charnel ground imagery.

What unlocks the appropriate palace gates in the end, so that she can access esoteric teachings, is an act of generosity. Left by her dakini guide, Yeshé Tsogyal approaches a palace where she must offer a tiger head to gain entrance. In search of a corpse, she comes upon a hungry tigress and her cubs, akin to the famous jataka tale but with a different resolution. Rather than sacrifice her life, Yeshé Tsogyal cuts off pieces of her own flesh to feed them, and the tigress returns the favor by helping her to locate the head of a deceased tiger.* Offering this allows her entrance into the palace, where various vidyadharas or "awareness holders" (*rig 'dzin*) dwell with their retinues and bestow on her a series of tantric initiations. Moreover, at the end of her twelve-year retreat, Padmasambhava returns to teach her the essential points of Dzogchen or the Great Perfection (*rdzogs chen*) in an extended dialogue. Her final act of generosity comes after receiving and realizing a host of profound teachings from Padmasambhava. In the final test prior to enlightenment, she is asked to rescue the evil minister Shanti(pa) from one of the realms of hell and, proving more than worthy, she liberates the entire realm through her meditative prowess.

Given the esoteric nature of this work and portions of Taksham's version, how might Yeshé Tsogyal serve as a female exemplar? In one significant way, she has provided an authoritative female antecedent for a number of women in the Nyingma tradition identified as her emanations.† Her legacy has thereby opened a cultural space for Tibetan women's entry into esoteric circles and,

---

* Elizabeth Angowski has done a nuanced analysis of this episode in a paper, "Intimate Relationships in the Early Lives of Yeshé Tsogyel," on the panel, *Female Lives and Narratives in Tibet: New Materials and New Perspectives*, at the Annual Meeting of the American Academy of Religion in Atlanta, November 21–24, 2015.

† This is particularly the case for Taksham's more well-known version of her life. Khandro Taré Lhamo's life story, *Spiraling Vine of Faith* (*Dad pa'i 'khri shing*), excerpts the sixth chapter of Taksham's version in the long preamble to her birth (Gayley 2016). Moreover, Sarah Jacoby highlights the intertextuality between Sera Khandro's autobiography and Taksham's version of Yeshé Tsogyal's life (2014: 87–91).

in certain cases, their recognition as teachers in their own right. Take for example the contemporary female master Khandro Taré Lhamo,* who received prophecies at birth identifying her with Yeshé Tsogyal. Compassion and tantric prowess are also central themes in her life story, which depicts Taré Lhamo rescuing locals from famine and other calamities of the Maoist period as well as from the ravages of hell. Other eminent female teachers who have been identified as emanations of Yeshé Tsogyal include Mingyur Paldrön (eighteenth century),† Terdak Lingpa's daughter, who supervised the reconstruction of Mindrolling Monastery in central Tibet after its destruction by the Dzungar Mongols, and the Treasure Revealer Sera Khandro (early twentieth century),‡ who fled her elite upbringing in Lhasa to follow her guru and destined consort Drimé Öser to the rugged landscape of Golok. Setting the stage for these identifications, both Drimé Kunga's and Taksham's renderings of her life contain predictions that Yeshé Tsogyal will continue to emanate across the generations in different regions of Tibet.

More generally, Yeshé Tsogyal serves as a model of spiritual attainment in female form. In Drimé Kunga's version, her forthright character, strong voice in opposing marriage, bravery in facing hardship, tenacity in pursuing the highest teachings, and compassion even toward her enemies are all exemplary. Yet Padmasambhava suggests that attaining enlightenment may be more challenging for a woman, even one like Yeshé Tsogyal with great

---

* See my study of Khandro Taré Lhamo's life and tantric partnership with Namtrul Rinpoche, *Love Letters from Golok: A Tantric Couple in Modern Tibet* (2016). My translation of their biographical corpus and correspondence are forthcoming with Shambhala Publications.

† Alison Melnick illuminates her life as an example of unprecedented female leadership in *The Life and Times of Mingyur Peldron: Female Leadership in 18th Century Tibetan Buddhism* (Ph.D. Dissertation, University of Virginia, 2014).

‡ Sarah Jacoby analyzes the auto/biographical writings of Sera Khandro in *Love and Liberation: Autobiographical Writings of the Tibetan Buddhist Visionary* (2014).

courage and determination. Is this a tacit acknowledgment of social conditions or a repetition of a well-worn stereotype? Either way, this caveat is set up to be overcome within the work itself. Although it might be disheartening to find denigrating comments toward women peppered throughout the secret biography, these are stereotypes that Yeshé Tsogyal clearly defies. As a disciple, she is given ample respect by Padmasambhava, who refers to her as a faithful woman and worthy recipient of tantric teachings. By the end of the story, in recognition of her realization, he refers to Yeshé Tsogyal as a "peerless dakini" (*mtshungs med mkha' 'gro*) comparable in manifestation to the primordial female buddha Samantabhadri (in the translation, "Buddha Lady Ever-Excellent"). In a salient twist, Padmasambhava states that his own good qualities come from Yeshé Tsogyal and not the other way around.

Recently, there has been a resurgence of interest in Yeshé Tsogyal as new sources come to light and as Tibetans create novel anthologies of works by and about eminent Buddhist women. Indicating her importance as an inspiration to female tantrikas (*sngags ma*), Yeshé Tsogyal and her emanations, mentioned above, were featured in a special issue of *The Journal for Research on Tantric Adepts* (2003), published in Xining, China.* More recently, Larung Buddhist Academy, a prominent Buddhist institution in eastern Tibet with a sizable population of monks and nuns, compiled a sixteen-volume collection, *A Garland of White Lotuses: The Liberation Stories of the Great Holy Women of India and Tibet* (2013).† It contains a treasure trove of material on Buddhist women, with most of one volume dedicated to Yeshé Tsogyal, and shows the ongoing relevance of recovering Buddhist women from the

---

* *Sngags pa'i shes rigs dus deb* 5:1 (2003). Under a mural image of Yeshé Tsogyal, reproduced in the journal, the caption refers to her as "Tibet's original female tantrika" (*bod kyi sngags ma thog ma*).

† *'Phags bod kyi skyes chen ma dag gi rnam par thar ba pad ma dkar po'i phreng ba*, edited by the Bla rung ar ya tA re dpe tshogs rtsom sgrig khang (Lha sa: Bod ljongs bod yig dpe rnying dpe skrun khang, 2013). Most of volume 6 is dedicated to Yeshé Tsogyal.

historical record to inspire female practitioners today. Following in Gyatso's footsteps, Elizabeth Angowski is crafting a literary analysis of Drimé Kunga's work and its intertextual resonances, and Jue Liang is tracing the different textual layers in the evolution of Yeshé Tsogyal's life story through a range of manuscripts now available. So this is an auspicious moment for the publication of Chönyi Drolma's eminently readable translation of *The Supreme Secret Biography of Yeshé Tsogyal, Chief Dakini*, allowing English readers to glimpse the multifaceted dimensions of this celebrated female figure in Tibetan Buddhism.

HOLLY GAYLEY is assistant professor of Buddhist Studies at the University of Colorado, Boulder, and author of *Love Letters from Golok: A Tantric Couple in Modern Tibet* (Columbia University Press, 2016). Her research focuses on the revitalization of Buddhism in Tibetan areas of the People's Republic of China in the post-Maoist period.

SOURCES CITED

Dowman, Keith. *Sky Dancer: The Secret Life and Songs of the Lady Yeshe Tsogyel*. Ithaca, NY: Snow Lion Publications, 1996.

Gayley, Holly. *Love Letters from Golok: A Tantric Couple in Modern Tibet*. New York: Columbia University Press, 2016.

Gross, Rita. "Yeshe Tsogyel: Enlightened Consort, Great Teacher, Female Role Model." In *Feminine Ground: Essays on Women in Tibet*, edited by Janice Willis, 11-32. Ithaca, NY: Snow Lion Publications, 1987.

Gyatso, Janet. *Apparitions of the Self: The Secret Autobiographies of a Tibetan Visionary*. Princeton: Princeton University Press, 1998.

Gyatso, Janet. "A Partial Genealogy of the Lifestory of Ye shes mtsho rgyal." *Journal of the International Association of Tibetan Studies*, no. 2 (August 2006): 1–27, www.thlib.org?tid=T2719.

Jacoby, Sarah. *Love and Liberation: Autobiographical Writings of the Tibetan Buddhist Visionary Sera Khandro*. New York: Columbia University Press, 2014.

Klein, Anne. *Meeting the Great Bliss Queen: Buddhists, Feminists, and the Art of the Self*. Boston: Beacon Press, 1994.

Padmakara Translation Group (trans.). *Lady of the Lotus-Born: The Life and Enlightenment of Yeshe Tsogyal*. Boston: Shambhala Publications, 1999.

Tarthang Tulku. *Mother of Knowledge: The Enlightenment of Yeshe Tsogyal*. Berkeley: Dharma Publishing, 1983.

Uebach, Helga. "Ladies of the Tibetan Empire, Seventh to Ninth Centuries CE." In *Women in Tibet*, edited by Janet Gyatso and Hanna Havnevik, 29–48. New York: Columbia University Press, 2005.

IMAGES OF SACRED PLACES AND OBJECTS FROM YESHÉ TSOGYAL'S LIFE

In 2007, I began the task of identifying the sacred places of Yeshé Tsogyal's life story in central Tibet. My hope was to go on a pilgrimage to these places, if at all possible.

Finally, in 2009, with the help of Professor Gyurme Dorje and his travel company, the journey materialized. Several sites were by no means on the trodden path and some caves and artifacts were photographed, perhaps for the first time, by Westerners. It is with great joy that Jnanasukha Foundation now offers this pilgrimage almost every year.

I offer my prayers that these photos, taken over the years, will enliven and deepen your connection with Yeshé Tsogyal, a timeless female buddha.

Lama Dechen Yeshe Wangmo
Jnanasukha Foundation

Yeshé Tsogyal Samyé mural.

Lotus-Born Guru Samyé mural.

Drak Valley, Yeshé Tsogyal's birthplace.

Yeshé Tsogyal's fourteenth-century birth stupa, 2009.

A new stupa that now encloses the fourteenth-century stupa, 2010.

Tsogyal Latso (Life Force Lake of Tsogyal) is the most renowned of Yeshé Tsogyal's ecological legacies. At her birth, a small nearby stream spontaneously increased in size, inspiring her father to name her Tsogyal (Victorious Lake). The lake later became a visionary site for several spiritual masters and is still regarded today as a manifestation of Yeshé Tsogyal and an important pilgrimage destination.

Yeshé Tsogyal's life-force tree at her birthplace, Tsogyal Latso.

Named in honor of Yeshé Tsogyal, Jomo Karak, the Snow Peaks of the Lady, are located in Tsang overlooking the Tsangpo River. Yeshé Tsogyal once gathered three hundred of her best disciples here for intensive training and, whenever she passed through, she received homage and offerings from the people.

Onphu Taktsang, where Yeshé Tsogyal hid from her suitors.

Yeshé Tsogyal's cave hermitage at Onphu Taktsang.

View toward the Tsangpo River from Yeshé Tsogyal's southern cave hermitage at Chimpu.

Samyé (Beyond Imagination) was the epicenter of Yeshé Tsogyal's era and where she frequently played a dynamic role in the politics of the day. One story about her life at Samyé recounts how she defeated her opponents during the two-year Great Debate that established Tibet as a Buddhist land.

Yarlung Sheldrak, where Yeshé Tsogyal concealed treasure texts such as Pema Katang.

Shoto Tidro Terdrom, where Yeshé Tsogyal practiced austerities and energy yoga.

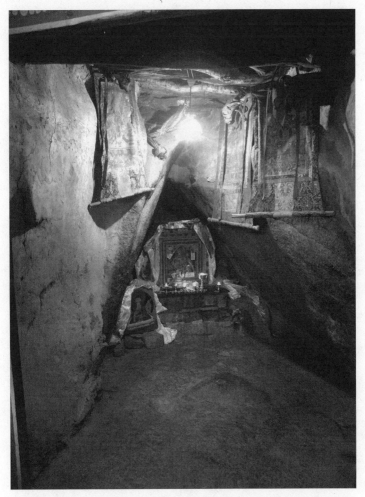

Yeshé Tsogyal's enlightenment cave at Zabbulung, where she attained the rainbow body.

Yeshé Tsogyal's stone handprint at Tsogyal Latso.

Yeshé Tsogyal's ritual dagger, or *phurba*, a rediscovered treasure at Zabbulung.

Yeshé Tsogyal Dechen Gyalmo statue at Tsogyal Latso.

The 108 rock piles at Zabbulung that each contain one bead of Yeshé Tsogyal's mala.

THE SUPREME SECRET
BIOGRAPHY OF YESHÉ TSOGYAL,
CHIEF DAKINI

TRANSLATOR'S INTRODUCTION

Yeshé Tsogyal—Queen of the Ocean of the Wisdom of Enlightenment—is the best-known and best-loved female Buddhist master in Tibetan Buddhism. This is her story, the autobiography of a princess born in eighth-century Tibet who became one of its foremost saints. She calls it the "secret" version of her life. By her standards, she invites us into her most personal space as she follows the Buddha's path, step for step. They each renounced their royal birthright, spent years in extreme hardship in spiritual practice, and attained enlightenment, to become known forevermore—somewhat ironically for an ex-prince and ex-princess—as "Lord of Sages" and "Queen of Wisdom," respectively.

This book allows us to accompany Yeshé Tsogyal as her secret confidante, to ford with her the valleys of her fears and failures, and to scale the peaks of her hopes and successes. She wrote this book to be accessible whether you read her words in translation out of curiosity or to nourish your established meditation practice. Her presentation is primarily narrative: she shares her experiences as they come, inviting us to explore and learn with her.

I have the tremendous good fortune of having been asked to translate this book. Although in a million lifetimes I could not do justice to Yeshé Tsogyal's own words, the impossible task of serving as her translator is straightforward enough: write in English as best I can what and how she wrote in Tibetan. Writing a "translator's introduction" to this book is far trickier. Some of you are new visitors to her world, some of you are longtime residents. Here is what I imagine might be useful to everyone as an introduction: first, a glimpse of her lasting legacy beyond the confines of this autobiography; second, a short account of how this book came to exist in its original Tibetan form; and last, overviews of each chapter.

Whether or not you generally read introductions, I strongly recommend visiting these chapter overviews. Why? Yeshé Tsogyal seems to have crafted each chapter as a unique jewel, quite distinctive in format and content from its neighbors. My intention is to offer you some context to help you immerse yourself in each chapter and to transition more easily between them.

One last word: at heart, the book you hold belongs to a genre, referred to in Buddhist languages as "a tale of freedom." Such autobiographies (or biographies) of enlightened masters are highly valued and quite popular, as they offer both instruction and inspiration. They are not meant to be read as histories. True to its genre, Yeshé Tsogyal's story invites us to follow her lead, to write our own tale of freedom, and to make the most of our life, dilemmas, and opportunities, just as she did.

THE LEGACY OF YESHÉ TSOGYAL

In her lifetime, Yeshé Tsogyal assumed a variety of exceptional roles to ensure that Buddhism would endure and flourish. She accomplished more than hundreds of lives or volumes can hold, and continues to do so throughout her endless emanations to the present.

First, as a historical figure, she was a model disciple. Her unwavering faith in her spiritual master and companion, Guru Rinpoche, was constant throughout her life. This devotion to the spiritual master (*lama* in Tibetan) is the art that is so central to tantric Buddhism's unique and swift effectiveness. Suffice it to say that if you're looking for an ideal role model, someone who demonstrated how to be an excellent disciple who aimed for and attained enlightenment in one lifetime, you've found her. This life story is her manual.

Any account, however detailed, of Yeshé Tsogyal's life amounts to just the beginning of her story. We are far removed from eighth-century Tibet, where we meet her, but Yeshé Tsogyal continues to be present and available. She lives outside linear time, but visits it: her limitless emanations form a bridge from her lifetime to the present. She promised to remain accessible to any spiritual seeker wishing to follow her lead. In her own words,

> And so, from now until the scouring of samsara,
> My stream of emanations, primary and secondary,
> Will flow unceasing.
> Especially to those who in the future meditate
> Upon the subtle veins and energies,
> I'll show myself—at best directly,
> Else in visions, or at least in dreams,
> Appearing as a common person, or as the secret consort.
> I shall clear the obstacles of those who keep samaya,
> Bringing progress to their practice,
> Helping to attain with speed the blissful warmth and
>   thence accomplishment.*

As promised, she continuously appears to lead and inspire the faithful in dreams, visions, and real life. As well, her human reincarnations ceaselessly return to the world, guiding others in whatever capacity is needed. This aspect of her legacy is so central that Guru Rinpoche spends much of the last two chapters of this book detailing her future emanations.

Where can we find them? Or how will they find us? It's somewhat ironic that although her reincarnations are endless and play crucial roles in the lives and lineages they touch, Yeshé Tsogyal remains very much an undercover agent, often "appearing as a common person."

I would suggest that this is less a form of humility than utter practicality. As we see in her story, Yeshé Tsogyal spent her entire life getting the job done. To the present day, she continues to do so largely free of the conventions, responsibilities, and constraints

* Changchub and Nyingpo 1999: 195.

that accompany official status in religious institutions. At the end of her life, she reminded her grieving disciples that she has always been "wild and fit for any deed." Then she made it clear to everyone how they can connect with her many, far-flung future emanations: "Those with faith, I, Tsogyal, never leave. For when you pray to me, I will be with you certainly."*

In Buddhism, we aspire to eventually serve both Buddhism itself and beings (including humanity). These two domains are not mutually exclusive, but it might seem that Yeshé Tsogyal's incarnations have been relegated to helping beings, while the service of Buddhism is the territory of males. If we measure Buddhism by walls and roofs, thrones and VIP seating, that would be true. Yet when we take refuge in the Dharma, we remind ourselves that it consists of scripture and realization, which in the Nyingma tradition is Queen Yeshé Tsogyal's realm. During her lifetime, she put into practice, accomplished, and conveyed every teaching she received. This includes the immense task of remembering, recording, and concealing the teachings known as "Treasures," the lifeblood of the Nyingma tradition. According to *The Life Stories of the Hundred Treasure Revealers*,

> Yeshé Tsogyal gathered all the inconceivable secret teachings given by Guru Rinpoche.... Much of the concealment of his teachings as Treasure texts was accomplished by this wisdom dakini. Her activity is boundless. She has continued to guide, give prophecies to, empower, and reassure great Treasure Revealers, and has emanated as consorts for many of them. Her direct emanations also include great women Treasure Revealers, who departed for the celestial realm without leaving their physical bodies behind. These include Jomo Memo and Dakini Kunga Bum. As shown, she is inconceivably amazing.†

* Ibid., 199.
† Kongtrul 2007: 381.

When Buddhists gather in public institutional settings, Yeshé Tsogyal (as a historical figure or in reincarnate human form) is often overlooked or given a seat by the door. When the same Buddhists receive private instruction and then sit alone to attain enlightenment, it is another matter entirely.

If I can interject my experience of Tibetan Buddhism, my home tradition (the New Treasures of Düdjom) occupies a small corner of the Nyingma. Despite the presence in the twentieth century of great female masters of our tradition, including Sera Khandro, Kunzang Wangmo, and Taré Lhamo, at this time most Düdjom temples, monasteries, and centers are led by men. Yet to a man, their spiritual lives are centered on Yeshé Tsogyal as much as on Guru Rinpoche; they are seen as inseparable, living presences to be sought in dreams, visions, meditative experiences, pilgrimage sites, and in real life.

THE JOURNEY OF YESHÉ TSOGYAL'S AUTOBIOGRAPHY

In her lifetime, Yeshé Tsogyal and Guru Rinpoche cofounded Tibet's Treasure tradition. Treasures are a form of spiritual technology that comprise one of tantric Buddhism's main forms of transmission. Simply put, it is a network that facilitates the preservation and delivery of sacred teachings and relics, often over the course of many centuries. It preserves relics and invaluable teachings, keeping them safe and pristine until their appropriate audience is ready to receive them, wherever and whenever they are needed. Although Yeshé Tsogyal does not mention this part of her life in the autobiography, it occupies a central place in her lifetime and legacy.

Let us use this autobiography as an example. In the eighth century, one of Guru Rinpoche's twenty-five main disciples, Bendé Sangyé Yeshé, asked Yeshé Tsogyal to tell him her life story. The result of that request, this present autobiography, was composed and concealed by Yeshé Tsogyal as an "earth Treasure"; that is to say, among the many kinds of Treasures, this one was a material object concealed in the physical terrain.

Five centuries later, a reincarnation of Bendé Sangyé Yeshé by the name of Drimé Kunga was born in Tibet in 1357. Drimé Kunga's career as a revealer of concealed Treasures began while he lived in retreat at Chimpu, the same place where most of Yeshé Tsogyal's life story took place.

> In Chimpu, at the top of Official's Neck Peak, Drimé Kunga received a prophecy from Guru Rinpoche; Yeshé Tsogyal gave him a list of Treasures he was to reveal. Based on those, in the next year he revealed a great number of Treasures, both sacred teachings and wealth practices. . . . He stayed in Chimpu practicing his Treasure revelations until signs of accomplishment arose.*

Drimé Kunga decided not to teach or spread the Treasures he unearthed. Instead, thinking of future generations, he reconcealed the texts in a cliff. Although this behavior might seem contradictory, it is not unusual. The meticulous process of Treasure concealment, revelation, and propagation is a delicate one. It depends on a great number of factors, including an appropriate revealer, a consort (an emanation of Yeshé Tsogyal herself in most cases), an auspicious time and place, and the presence of qualified recipients. If the circumstances are not conducive, a Treasure Revealer will return the teachings to their bank for safekeeping, for another, better time.

Such is the case for this book. In 1848, Drimé Kunga's Treasures found the great master Jamyang Khyentsé Wangpo (1820–1892) during a journey between Lhasa and Chimpu.

> In the vicinity of the temple, a woman approached to offer Jamyang Khyentsé Wangpo a [clay] finger [rescued] from a collapsed giant Buddha statue, which he put in the fold of his robe and continued on his way, forgetting meanwhile

---

* Ibid., 559–61.

that it was even there. Later on when changing his clothes, as he loosened the belt of his robe it fell to the ground, and on inspection he saw that the finger had broken, and inside were the Treasure scrolls . . . that had been reconcealed by Drimé Kunga.*

Some of Drimé Kunga's Treasures that were recovered by Khyentsé were then added to the encyclopedic compendium called *The Vault of Valuable Treasures*. It seems that this one was not, although a woodblock was made of this text at some point after 1848. About one hundred fifty years after its second discovery, in 1996, Professor Janet Gyatso found a copy of the woodblock print at the Public Library of Lhasa in central Tibet. She subsequently offered it to Khenchen Palden Sherab Rinpoche. He proofread and edited the recently produced digital version of the Tibetan text that was used for this translation.

Several years ago, the head of the Jnanasukha Foundation, Lama Dechen Yeshe Wangmo, received this Tibetan edition. We began discussing the translation in June 2015. After a century and a half, including several disappearances and recoveries, how fortuitous to finally have an English-language translation in one's hands! Without a doubt, Yeshé Tsogyal has been present at every step along the way. I hope this book serves as an opportunity to meet her, to learn from her, and to follow her lead.

Chönyi Drolma

---

* Kongtrul 2012: 139.

Sources Cited

Tibetan Works

Jamgön Kongtrul. (Kong sprul blo gros mtha' yas, 1813–1899). *The Life Stories of the Hundred Treasure Revealers* (*Gter ston rgya rtsa*). In Vol. 1 (Ka) of *The Vault of Valuable Treasures* (*Rin chen gter dzod chen mo*), Shechen Edition, 2007.

English Translations

Jamgön Kongtrul. *The Life of Jamyang Khyentse Wangpo.* Translated by Matthew Akester. New Delhi: Shechen Publications, 2012.

Gyalwa Changchub and Namkhai Nyingpo. *Lady of the Lotus-Born: The Life and Enlightenment of Yeshe Tsogyal.* Translated by the Padmakara Translation Group. Boston: Shambhala Publications, 1999.

Chapter Overviews

Chapter 1: Palace Life and Strife

This first chapter, in which Yeshé Tsogyal shares the trials of her early life prior to meeting Guru Rinpoche, is full of conflicts. It raises questions pertinent to many modern Buddhists born outside of native Buddhist contexts. For instance, have you ever felt like you were born into the wrong family, the wrong society, and possibly even the wrong body? Imagine dealing with the expectations to perform, succeed, and conform in a way that makes sense within a tradition and community and yet has nothing to do with what's inside you. Now add the pressure of a being part of a royal family, in which one's status is both a crown jewel and an expensive bartering piece.

Chapter 1 describes just this. We see how Yeshé Tsogyal is born into a wealthy and powerful Tibetan royal family amid miraculous signs, which her Buddhist family ultimately ignores. Her displays of extraordinary spiritual qualities from a young age are also devalued. Instead, the political officials in her palace view her as a highly marketable pawn, princes of various nationalities find her irresistible, and she's saddled with a very large dowry. This can only lead to trouble.

When it does, the events that unfold are consistently ghastly and terrible. Yeshé Tsogyal's early life, until meeting Guru Rinpoche and entering retreat, is quite frankly traumatic. Her birth into a Buddhist family, kingdom, and country did nothing to help her spiritual path. In fact, she may have inherited more obstacles to spiritual practice than many of us! Whatever the case, in the end, having given up and lost everything, even her dignity, she pursued her path, met her spiritual master, and escaped. And that's all that really matters, then or now.

CHAPTER 2: VISIONARY VOYAGES

With the second chapter, the fun really begins. The secret aspect of her autobiography comes to the fore. What distinguishes a secret account from outer and inner narratives is the depth to which we are granted access to a person's life. Here, Yeshé Tsogyal begins to experience and share her inner transformation, catalyzed by finally meeting her lama and companion, Guru Rinpoche. Most importantly, these episodes illustrate the often arduous stages of her awakening process. This chapter begins as she enters twelve years of retreat at Chimpu and miraculously journeys to the lands of Oddiyana.

Many of the key episodes in Oddiyana have to do with the transmissions that are central to tantric Buddhism. These essential transmissions fall into three categories. First, empowerments are given by qualified masters to suitable disciples in order to initiate them into a specific practice, teaching, or deity meditation. In this chapter, Yeshé Tsogyal receives many empowerments, both during formal rituals and in more spontaneous interactions.

Second, scriptural transmissions take place when a sacred text is recited aloud by an individual who has previously received the same transmission. The act of hearing the words formally grants disciples permission to read and learn from the text. This also creates a connection to receive the blessings of its meaning and the lineage behind it. Such a reading would likely precede all the doctrinal cycles she receives in the fourth chapter.

Third, after disciples lay these foundations to prepare their minds, they then receive the transmission of teachings and sacred advice that lead to insight and liberation. Yeshé Tsogyal receives such counsel throughout her life. This is especially true during the challenges she faces in Oddiyana in the second chapter, and throughout her discourse with Guru Rinpoche in the third chapter.

It's noteworthy that the types of tantric transmissions she received have not changed in substance since her lifetime. The setting might be different, but how and why they are conveyed remain the same. The importance of this process cannot be emphasized enough, and no degree of stature or experience on the part of the practitioner makes them optional. There are many fascinating stories of lamas spending months or years receiving the teachings they themselves composed during previous lifetimes.

The second chapter is also where we see Yeshé Tsogyal confronted with her own shortcomings, both as a person and as a practitioner. During her adventures in the strange lands of Oddiyana, she is challenged to examine herself. She rarely measures up and, to her own dismay, often fails. In return for her perseverance, she receives the same core teachings on faith, impermanence, and courage that are so essential for anyone intent on awakening. Although her outer experiences—intense, fantastical, and sometimes bizarre—are unique to her story and likely exotic to us, readers are once again invited to relate to her inner journey. Her visionary voyages contain the same elements of challenge, self-evaluation, and growth that all practitioners must be ready for in order to progress along the spiritual path.

CHAPTER 3: SUBLIME QUESTIONS AND ANSWERS

In chapter 3, Yeshé Tsogyal shares with us an extraordinary series of teachings received from Guru Rinpoche. They cover the entire Buddhist path and provide answers to timelessly relevant questions for aspiring meditators at all stages. The subjects include: What sort of lama should I accept as my spiritual guide? What should my spiritual companions be like? How do I handle dying? How can I overcome obstacles? Who can attain enlightenment?

While this advice is both sublime and practical, a lot of information is presented here. Several lamas who helped me with this translation said this of the third chapter: "These teachings are complete and extraordinary, but some are also extremely condensed. Longer explanations can be found elsewhere." As readers, this advice is important to keep in mind. These passages often address deep subjects in a concise manner. In certain cases, Guru Rinpoche employs metaphors or even codes to represent more esoteric subjects. Such allusions will be familiar to disciples already qualified to put these teachings into practice. As for the rest of us, they may seem cryptic, and that's perfectly fine.

CHAPTER 4: TEACHINGS AND POSTERITY

Chapter 4 steps back from the narrative format to present readers with a comprehensive list of teachings that Yeshé Tsogyal received in her lifetime. It is worth recalling the first line of this entire book, in which we are told that she possessed perfect memory. This ability allowed her to miraculously retain every teaching and every detail Guru Rinpoche conveyed. She went on to master these teachings and, in many cases, to catalog, encode, and conceal them as Treasures for the sake of their later revelation by and for future disciples.

CHAPTER 5: TO HELL AND BACK

Yeshé Tsogyal's next story is a wild ride. Approached by a creature from hell challenging her to help others, she naïvely asks him in which pure land (a heaven-like paradise conducive to spiritual practice) her disciples are waiting. He tells her to go to hell. She does, using her training to bravely traverse its levels of karmically prescribed torture and pain in pursuit of an individual closely related to her traumatic youth.

The fifth chapter is pivotal because, at its conclusion, Yeshé Tsogyal finally receives the name by which she is known: Dakini Yeshé Tsogyal. This investiture is especially moving once we learn its deeper meaning. The hell-being who commends and names her employs an element of Tibetan literature that is somewhat difficult to express in translation. He uses each syllable of her name to spell out her exceptional qualities. Its meaning is so profound that he chooses a homonym to give one syllable a double meaning: "nourishes" in the description and "ocean" in the actual spelling of her name. In an attempt to share how this key passage looks in its original Tibetan form, I've added bold emphasis to the translated syllables of her name, in addition to giving the Tibetan transliteration.

> You've gained mastery of realization. In the **space** (*mkha'*) of the nature of reality, you **move** (*'gro*) with the force of the **wisdom** (*ye shes*) of awareness. Your nondual compassion **nourishes** (*'tsho*) beings and is **victorious** (*rgyal*) over all suffering. Therefore, your nondual compassion is stronger than that of all peaceful and wrathful triumphant buddhas, including Lord Heruka. I give you the name **Dakini** (*mkha' 'gro*) **Yeshé** (*ye shes*) **Tsogyal** (*mtsho rgyal*), **Victorious Ocean of Wisdom**.

Chapters 6 and 7: Prophecies as Bridge to the Present

The book concludes with two chapters focused on Guru Rinpoche's prophecies and practical instructions for Yeshé Tsogyal. In the sixth chapter, he describes her successive incarnations and commands her to launch her career as curator of the Treasure tradition. She is largely responsible for all the Treasures that have reached the present day.

In the seventh chapter, Yeshé Tsogyal asks for further clarification to Guru Rinpoche's previous instructions. He responds with a broader view of who and what is to come. These disturbingly accurate prophecies describe both our world and the future state of the sacred doctrine.

1: The Birth and Early Life of the Princess

Namo Guru Deva Dakini Ye
Homage to the Lama Goddess Dakini

I bow to great bliss,
Buddha Lady Ever-Excellent.
I bow to the ultimate formless dimension of enlightenment,
Buddha Infinite Illumination.
I bow to enlightenment's form dimension of complete enjoyment,
Buddha Supreme Compassion.
I bow to enlightenment's form dimension of manifest
    embodiment,
Lama Lotus-Born.
I bow to these deities
of enlightenment's changeless three dimensions.

I, Yeshé Tsogyal, an emanation of the awakened heroine Melodi-ous [Sarasvati], who possess perfect and unfailing memory, com-posed this account of my life to foster all future beings' interest in the teachings and practice of the sacred doctrine.

The dominion of Tibet is the Land of Snows; at its heart stood a large town called Yaru Drak. It was equal to the Indian town of Bheta, adorned with many virtues. North of the magnificent town of Yaru Drak stood many forests of red and white sandalwood, as well as eaglewood trees. These stretched in every direction around a pleasant grove of trees transplanted from the bodhi tree [under which Shakyamuni Buddha attained enlightenment].

In that grove grew a garden of white lotuses and water lilies. At its center rose a beautiful and lavishly adorned palace called Lukar Gardens. Its riches were equal to those of the Heaven of the Thirty-Three. Countless people, including a royal court and servants, lived there.

The king and queen were called Lord Vajra Recall and Lady Accomplisher of Inner Luminosity. Theirs was a noble family line with great power. The king and queen bore two princes and seven princesses. Yeshé Tsogyal was the youngest of the seven girls and was called Princess Lady Lotus. She was easygoing, disciplined, and noble in her bearing. Her speech was melodious. An attractive and pleasing sight to see, her resplendent body was radiant. She spoke sweet words and her mind always brimmed with compassion.

Her body bore all the marks and signs of physical perfection; she had every positive quality. Her outward form was that of an excellent dakini, a manifest embodiment of enlightenment. Inwardly, she was Dakini Vajra Sow, and secretly, Buddha Ever-Excellent's dakini display.

She possessed every characteristic of the three dimensions of enlightenment, fully present of their own accord. Although her wisdom mind rested in the expanse of the nature of reality, she assumed the two form dimensions of enlightenment in order to help others.

Encouraged by the buddhas' nondual compassion, as well as the momentum of her own aspirations, the princess entered her queen mother's blissful womb. In the first month of spring during the Earth Rat Year, she was born on the morning of the tenth day. The people around her saw clear evidence of her previous acts and qualities. Without a doubt, they were confident that she had every characteristic of an exceptional individual. Her remarkable acts caused them great delight. She had a way about her.

A month after conceiving, the queen's dreams, experiences, and waking life were filled with dakinis: multitudes of white women bathed her; blue women scattered flowers around her; yellow women offered her nectar; red women adorned her with jewelry; and green women circumambulated her. Many sixteen-year-old girls at the height of youth surrounded the queen. Late at night, she constantly heard sounds of supplications.

A month after the princess was born, light encircled the infant's body to an arm-span's distance; her speech naturally resounded with spiritual teachings; and her mind remained in evenness within clear light. At eight months old, every morning she would enter a canopy of rainbows and light. At night, she played with a group of young dakinis.

When she was one year old, many young girls and boys gathered around her and she granted them empowerments, including one called "Unsurpassable Array pure land." She lived in the constant enjoyment of great bliss.

At the age of eight, the princess showed many signs of clair-voyance and displayed miraculous acts, by which she revealed to others the nature of all things. When she was eleven, she taught extensively on the doctrines of the tantras. Her great intelligence, conduct, and joyful manner brought many of her land's subjects under her influence.

When the princess turned sixteen, the king of Bhijara in India decided that she should marry his son. He sent an ambassador to her palace, who addressed the royal family, court, and subjects with these words: "Hear ye! King and Queen, court, and subjects. I ask you all to pay heed. This princess of yours would be a fitting queen for our Indian king. Therefore, if you find it suitable to send her, I implore you, King, grant your permission."

In response, the king, queen, princes, officials, and subjects consulted and came to an agreement. The king proclaimed:

> Pay heed! This girl, Princess Lotus,
> has every positive quality.
> No one but a prince may marry her.
> We give our consent

to send her to marry your king's son.
That said, you, my state officials,
should come to an agreement
and have her depart with her dowry.

The state officials announced:

Although she is a delightful girl,
she shouldn't stay in her homeland.
The people of India are excellent.
This girl should marry the Indian prince
and become his queen!

We officials will escort her a short way.
It would be best if she lived in India.
However, if the girl refuses to go,
she will be punished by her older brothers
for disobeying her parents' royal command.

The domestic officials stated:

This princess is amazing! She is magnificent!
As for the matter of sending her far away,
does this really strike us as something good?
If she departs involuntarily,
this land will lose its good fortune.
Instead of being wed at a distance,
it would be better if she married a local man.

She should stay here in our own land of Tibet,
where the court and subjects can care for her.
King, Queen, and state officials,
we beg you to grant your permission
for her to stay in Tibet.

However, if you ignore our counsel
and she is barred from staying here,
when the princess is sent to India,
we domestic officials will all follow after her.

The princes and the queen should meet and discuss this,
examining the question,
"May the princess remain here with the Tibetan people?"
If she cannot stay,
this concludes our advice on this matter.

They announced this together in complete accord.
  In response to the question posed, the queen replied:

My daughter is a princess with every positive quality.
I cannot bear to part with her:
do not send her away to India!
She should stay here in Tibet,
in our very own land.

One highborn girl is superior to any prince.
If you don't dismiss her
to that frightening land of bandits,
she can stay here in the palace for some years.

That is my prayer;
you will surely grant my wish!

The pair of princes gave their answer:

Our sister is a captivating princess,
exceptionally endowed with the best qualities.
However, she should not stay here in her homeland—
we agree she should go marry elsewhere.

This realm of Tibetans is a desert,
devoid of qualities,
the home of lowborn and wretched people.

Compare that to the glorious, noble land of India!
Source of all things joyous,
boasting ten thousand oceanic treasure vaults,
that place is filled with the five forms of wealth
and a bounty of pleasures.

The king of Bhijara is a descendant of the Shakya clan;
if the princess married into that family,
it would be wonderful!
We encourage her to do so quickly,
and the officials should escort her a short way.
Send her along with her dowry in the envoy's hand.

Throughout the town and palace, everyone was utterly miserable. They wailed aloud, lamenting:

Our princess is the source of all that is good in our lives,
a wish-fulfilling jewel that grants what we need and desire.
If she does not remain in Tibet because you send her away,
this land's very marrow will be sapped.
The rulers and their subjects will be devastated!
We will die!

All our good fortune will be lost at the borderland.
If the kingdom's merits are wasted,
how can it carry on?
For those reasons, we beseech you as one:
let her stay!
That said, if you ignore our request and send her to India,
all of us, her downcast subjects, will go with her.
Pay attention to our unanimous decision!

People agreed on the issue wholeheartedly. However, the subjects and court had little control over the matter and no power to keep her in Tibet. The formidable king, the two princes, and the state officials held all the authority. They promised to send the princess to India.

The prince of Bhijara sent five hundred mounted envoys, who offered five hundred gold coins as a tribute to the princess. The Indian envoys accepted her dowry in return—countless loads of gifts. A team of five hundred elephants was laden with food and supplies; another team carried clothing and jewelry; yet another bore jewels and such. Furthermore, her family offered a group of five hundred girls to adorn the princess with jewelry, another group to bathe her, another to serve her food, and yet another to handle her expensive goods. There were also five hundred serving boys, among thousands of others. Everyone was stationed at a garden meadow in the mountain forest.

On the fifteenth day of the third month of the Wood Rabbit Year, the commitment to send the princess and her dowry to India was finalized. At this point, an incarnate master skilled in astrology and divination came from western India. He used astrological calculations to determine the best time for the five hundred envoys to return with her to India. However, due to disturbances in the land, region, and natural elements, they never had a chance to leave. They promised to depart for India some years later.

East of Tsepo Podrang lived another king, named Radiant Moon. His palace, located on a wooded, sandy plain, was called Mighty Fortress of the Stream. That king and his son, Prince Bright White, had heard appealing words of praise concerning the princess's outstanding qualities.

In response, they entrusted five hundred officials with two hundred expensive containers of jewels for her. Sending these gift-bearing envoys, they also commissioned mediators and clever advisers who promised to carry out the prince's command.

When this group approached the princess directly, she read them a letter she had written for their prince:

Pay heed! These jeweled coffers make the king's will clear!
Although I am not worthy of this gesture,
we are connected through our previous aspirations,
so it is excellent that he sent these envoys with a pure
    intention.

Prince, I have no wrong impressions of you.
However, I, the princess, aspire only to do spiritual practice,
so I am returning each and every container of jewels.

As for all of your envoys,
I have quenched their thirst and relieved their hunger,
giving them food, drink, and supplies
to shelter them from unhappiness.

I offer you this aspiration:
may we meet in Unsurpassable pure land!

She placed this letter in a container to send back with his envoys, who returned home.

The Indian prince of Bhijara had also sent some wise and clever advisers among his envoys. They approached the princess discreetly, on the side, to offer her a container filled with highly coveted wealth. In response, the princess wrote a letter to their prince. She placed this in a box, entrusted his officials with its delivery, and had them return to their homeland. The letter read:

Greetings to you, Prince.
You are a descendent of the Buddhist Shakya clan;
the nectar of your goodness flows like a snow mountain
    river.
Your body has all the characteristics of physical
    perfection—
it is irresistible to behold.
The banner of your sweet voice reaches many lands.

You enjoy your circle of ladies in the dance of your youth,
as your radiant smile enraptures your court and subjects.

How excellent it would be to marry an awakened hero
    like you!
Although I'm in love with you and cannot bear us to be
    apart,
this princess aspires only to practice the spiritual teachings.

I will cultivate meditative stability
in an empty, deserted valley.
Dressed in tattered rags,
I will keep a humble position
and take sustenance from the elements
to feed my meditative stability.

I have no wish for nourishing food and drink.
I will cultivate meditative experience, heat, and bliss
within the fortress of my meditative stability.

A palace, court, and subjects are like a dream or magical
    illusion.
I seek isolation in the certainty that nothing can last or
    endure.

In this lifetime, I will not be connected to you as your wife.
In a future life, I aspire for us to meet in Unsurpassable
    pure land.

The prince was given the box that held her letter. The princess was
satisfied with her own response.

From the perspective of the soliciting princes, her people—the
king, as well as his princes and officials—had promised to give the
princess to them. One prince had sent containers of wealth as gifts,
yet she aspired to pursue practice. No matter the circumstances, the

princess had decided not to go near him. Nor would she consent to become anyone's queen. As for the envoys, they were ashamed and disappointed because they failed to deliver the princess.

Among her own people, her father, the king, and his officials, court, and subjects were all deeply unhappy. As it stood, the princess refused to go as ordered, even though her family had promised to send her. They had accepted the expensive tributes offered them. The envoys had been sent back to their own lands, where their rulers were certain to be offended.

At this point, the king, his subjects, and their lands would be defeated in war. Every ounce of their great wealth, stolen; the palace and all their homes, destroyed. The people of quality—officials and subjects—would be killed; the king and queen and their children, banished to another land. Even the princess herself would be powerless. The foreign rulers would seize and abduct her.

At this point, everyone was filled with despair and regret. "Now is the right time to discuss this with the princess," they decided unanimously.

The king addressed his state officials:

Pay heed! You officials are the ones
who failed to resolve this!
You are skilled at being divisive
with your grand mouths and big words.
Do not upset the princess with your harsh arguments.

Steer her away from those ten unwanted outcomes,
but be sure not to reveal what you're doing.
If she will not stay where we send her,
we in the palace will be enraged.
We will torment you officials in revenge,
so do what we agreed upon!

That was his command to the state officials.
They implored in turn:

Pay heed! King and princes,
you are angry because you are thinking of money,
though it is you who failed to send the dowry as payment
after you accepted their expensive gifts in bad faith.
You did not use your wealth to take care of them
and made a rash decision in poor judgment.

You failed to offer the prince all he desires,
so he is definitely not pleased.
If the kingdom seeking the marriage
loses what they gave us and what they came for,
they will become vindictive.
Where will the princess go if she has no food or wealth?
It is you, King, who must make a plan to satisfy their
     demands.

While that was happening, the princess thought to herself:

If I am unable to practice
in these moments when I think of it,
my life will be wasted in constant laziness.
That is why it is right to endure hardship
for the sake of putting the spiritual teachings into practice.
I will succeed in this matter
by being clever and deft.
My parents are good to me,
so I have to do all I can
to insistently seek their permission.

The princess approached her parents, earnestly imploring them:

Pay heed! I can never repay your care and kindness.
As you lovingly nurtured me,
my qualities blossomed.
Who is the kindest friend?

It is someone who follows the spiritual teachings.
Should it not contradict your wishes,
this is surely what I would do.
Then, my parents, your minds and lives will be happy.

I beg you to grant me permission
to freely undertake spiritual practice.
Were I to train in basic meditative stability,
joy and good fortune would come
to the royal family and all your subjects.
Please allow me to endure the hardship
of living in an empty, deserted valley.

Everyone, the royal family and officials alike, were united in
their opinion. Their faces darkened as they shook their fists. Each
person took a turn in making their blustering statements with
harsh words.

The king began:

Enthralling, superb, and wellborn princess,
I have joyfully cherished and cared for you
since you were young.

Now you are grown with a good life.
At this point, having gained independence,
you no longer obey your own father.

You will not go where we send you,
nor will you stay where we intend you to live.
There is a lovely town for you in India,
yet you fail to see its good points.
Princess, you are quite stupid!

That prince, his family, and their subjects
offered you expensive gifts,

yet you do not trust them.
Princess, you are very dim-witted!

The royal family, envoys, and subjects
endured great hardship for you.
You never gave them a second thought
when making your bad decision.

Despite all the fatherly kindness
I have shown you, Princess,
you never remember that goodness,
as you foolishly repay me with your dreadful behavior.

If you had a brain,
you would not defy my wishes!
Go to India, the source of your future happiness.

Then the queen spoke:

Pay heed! Captivating princess,
born of my own flesh,
it is not a small decision to disobey your mother.
You refuse to be sent away,
and I do not forget the meaning of those words.

While India is very far,
your other suitor lives nearby
in Mighty Fortress, a source of joy!
That palace itself is a treasure vault.
Married to that prince,
life will be good
and your fortune will not be lacking.
I would even give you
an inheritance from my own wealth.

Should you live in that palace,
magnificent joy would follow.
For the most part,
your practice will overcome everything,
and you will reign over your kingdom
according to spiritual ideals.
Do not be sad;
heed your mother's wishes!

The princes and state officials added:

Alas! Your self-regard
and sense of entitlement are quite high.
Princess, you are being stupid.
Listen to us!
When you ignored our advice
by refusing to go where we sent you,
you pushed your humble court and subjects into enemy hands.

You are not taking care of this happy kingdom
with your confused and worthless idea.
You claim you will wander in an empty valley:
don't count on that plan.
You should go to India!

In any case, it is a grave offense if you refuse to go.
If you had a brain,
you would look seriously at your decision.
Girls who don't listen
are a graveyard for their fathers and brothers.

Princess, if, by chance you will not go to India,
that foreign army will rout your father and brothers.
This realm and every resident will be crushed in defeat.
Every friendly ally will become the enemy's war god.

If you do not listen to our advice,
you will cause this kingdom's downfall.

Once you've given this proper thought,
we will give you food and wealth
without a moment's hesitation.
The king's officials will be your best supporters!
Should you succeed in this mission,
that's what will make you an intelligent princess.
Heed our counsel
and you will excel in whatever you please.

The princess thought to herself, "The king, officials, and subjects have a very negative attitude toward the sacred doctrine. They are such terrible people! Speaking harshly to them will not frighten them; yet if I ask calmly, they will just ignore me.

"I can part with my coveted expensive goods, including my turquoise jewelry. I'll divide and hand out my wealth to each and every person among the royal family, officials, court, and subjects. After setting this clever plan into motion, I must appeal to each of them resolutely, using soft words.

"I wonder if they will allow me to practice the spiritual teachings? Whatever I do, if they deny me the fortune to use this, a valuable human life I've gained for that purpose, I will offer my body and life before the palace shrine. After this lifetime, I pray and aspire to have the power to practice until awakening. This is the right thing to do. No matter what, I will use my strong character and fortitude to convince them."

The princess offered these items to her father, the king: a gold-and-turquoise hairpiece, agate-and-turquoise earrings, a pearl-and-turquoise necklace, and the radiant turquoise gem that she wore at the crown of her head. She gave her rings and a white-silver mirror to her brothers, the two princes. To her mother, the queen, the princess presented a soft, woven gown adorned with pearls, an exquisitely tailored brocade of the finest silk inlaid with turquoise, a statue with pearl ornaments, a dark-blue mother-of-pearl polishing cloth, a turquoise hairpiece with an intricate knot design, a golden knife, a scepter with a jeweled handle, and her turquoise shoes with a delicate upturned border.

To the state officials she bestowed a golden, turquoise-inlaid container of wealth with seven tiers. As for the domestic officials, court, and subjects, she presented them with a golden, turquoise-inlaid container of wealth with seven dangling strands of pearls.

For the masses of wretchedly poor among the lowest classes, and all those who were parched, starving, and utterly impoverished, the princess opened numerous smaller treasure chests. She offered each individual a rightful share of her possessions. In order to satisfy everyone, she even gave food and drink to the birds, dogs, and other animals.

The princess asked the king and queen, the princes, the state and domestic officials, and the court and subjects to gather in a large group at the foot of a tree shaped like a round lotus. Then, with much sadness and lamenting, she appealed to each of them in turn, clearly and sincerely. Every time she spoke, tears flowed like blood from her eyes. Her chest heaved with great gasps until she fainted, losing consciousness. First she addressed her father:

> How astonishing!
> My king and father,
> your words are your command,
> but I am not satisfied with that—
> this is my own fault.
> If I cannot pursue spiritual practice,
> my life is an empty waste!
>
> Karma is the cause of delusion,
> and my mind only perpetuates suffering.
> Everything that is the round of rebirth
> leaves me physically exhausted and mentally weary.
> Putting energy into mundane tasks is like ripples on water.

The spiritual teachings are what we need
for this life and the next.
I, this youthful princess,
have taken a low birth as a woman.
My every thought and experience
fuels my wish for these teachings.
Compelled by this intense longing,
I will bear hardship for the sake of practice.
The opulence and the people around me
cause the suffering
that we call the round of rebirth.
Even if I had a handsome prince for a husband,
I would merely be led by the appearance of something
    worthwhile.
Great fame only invites gossip.

Since I have no wish to remain
in the home of the karmic round of rebirth,
I implore you to listen,
my king and father:
do not send me to India.
When my spiritual practice comes to fruition,
your kindness as my father will be repaid in full.

That said, if you do not grant me permission
to put the spiritual teachings into practice,
that will be the end of this life for me
and I will pray to meet you in the next.

The princess beseeched her mother, the queen:

How astonishing!
You kindly created me from your own flesh—
that is our connection.
Karma led me to you as my mother.

Yet all the while you make a big show
of your deep love for me,
you are not really taking care of this princess.

The Buddha said, "If your parents aren't spiritual allies,
they side with demons and destructive forces."
Therefore, although you are strict,
I beg you to grant me permission
to fulfill my wish for spiritual practice.

The palace, wealth, and possessions are a mirage in space.
Turquoise jewelry and clothing are like honey to a bee.
For whoever craves those things,
they cause delusion.
I reject clinging and dualistic fixation;
I will practice the sacred teachings.
Mother, if you really can't honor my wish,
our relationship in this life is over;
I will make aspirations to meet you in the next
in Unsurpassable pure land.

The princess addressed her two brothers, the princes, as well as
the state officials:

How astonishing!
The momentum of karma has joined us;
our relationship is affectionate.
Yet even as you princes
and mighty officials scold me,
I, the princess, feel no woe or regret.

Since our thoughts and impressions
are self-created and different,
each person sees things subjectively
and experiences that corresponding karma.

In that far-off land of India,
the king of Bhijara roars in grievance;
his court and servants are rudely short-tempered.
Their wealth is difficult to guard and hold in its coffers;
they have to gauge the opinions
of their townspeople, spouses, subjects, and court;
their state and domestic officials are expert complainers;
it is difficult to manage rival kings and their officials.
Making the spiritual teachings disappear,
their king will lead everyone's lives into misery.
As the sun of the king sets,
the king of deluded darkness can begin his reign.

Every misfortune converges in a land like that—
I will not go live in such a place!
This princess is like a flower blossom.
The clear light of awareness will entirely fade
in that far-off realm of beasts.

Father, mother, and officials,
when I am far away and cannot see you,
my mind and outlook will slip into despair.
We share neither language nor ethnicity with them:
it would be like having beasts as companions!

Thinking all day and night of the palace,
their plotting officials are evil people
who would defeat my mind,
leaving this princess bleak.

This is why I beg you,
princes and officials,
to grant me permission to practice.
No matter the outcome,
if you punish me for trying,

this princess is ready to give up her life.
So while my body satisfies the aims
of you officials and subjects,
my mind wishes for us all to meet
in Unsurpassable pure land.

Since we are not able to be companions in this life,
I aspire for us to meet again in the future
through timely interdependent connections.

All of those permitted to attend the gathering—including
her parents, the king and queen, the princes, and the important
officials—reached the same conclusion. They announced:

No matter the circumstances,
the princess refuses to go to India
and we will not stand for this.

We have to send her to Mighty Fortress
to marry their prince!
If we offer them the wealth of her dowry,
which is not trivial,
she absolutely must go.

If she refuses this plan as well,
that is definitely a legal offense,
for which it is fitting to cut off her head and limbs.
Anyone friendly with the princess
who fears this outcome—
go reason with her insistently!

Having come to this agreement, they entrusted their message to
five hundred girls sympathetic to the princess. These girls then
addressed her:

Pay heed! You are an intelligent person,
a good product of your youth and upbringing.

The sight of your excellent clan, family line,
and character enthralls other people.
You have knowledge and intelligence,
as well as youth's physical signs and traits.

Listen to the wise king, officials, and subjects.
Although we love you, Princess,
do not disobey the king's command.
If you defy his orders,
the officials will punish you severely.

Therefore, if you don't listen to our advice
and refuse to live in India,
there is no way to avoid going to Mighty Fortress.
Based on those facts,
we beg you to give us a clear answer.

The princess responded to the five hundred girls and the other
counselors:

Alas! You five hundred girls are concerned friends
who approach me with great affection,
saying many things you consider helpful.

Yet as soon as we disagree even slightly,
you stop supporting me
and deviously lure me to your outcome.

I have no wish to be part of a royal household,
so take this permission to join the prince's palace
and do with it whatever makes you happy.

This princess will stay in the deserted snow mountains.
If I don't practice the spiritual teachings,
I should be severely punished!
I have definitely made my decision
and harbor no doubts in my mind.
Deliver that message to the king and officials.

After that, the five hundred girls who advised the princess recounted her words, with nothing added or omitted, to the king and queen, officials, and subjects. Everyone was shocked and enraged.

The state officials, who felt hostile toward the sacred doctrine, beseeched the king:

The king's law, which sustains the realm,
states that anyone's beloved child who is found guilty
can be put to death.
As for this precious princess whom you nurtured,
if she refuses to go where she is sent,
we will cut off her head,
flay her skin, and dismember her.
That is the suitable and lawful course of action.

Once they appealed to the king, he agreed and granted his permission to carry out this punishment.

After that, the crowd of corrupt officials seized the princess. They bound her arms behind her back, stripped her naked, and fastened a rope around her neck. Lashing her with a whip of thorns, they paraded her around the palace's perimeter. All the people of the realm wept at the sight of her, wailing loudly.

There was one domestic official, called Trena Kar, who was very ashamed of this situation. Quite wise and supportive of the spiritual teachings, he returned to the palace and confronted the king.

How astonishing!
What were you thinking
when you authorized this, my king?
As your offspring,
the princess is indispensable.
The corrupt officials manipulated you with divisive words!
Failing to use your judgment,
you placed her in the hands of the enemy.

Lacking any concern for the princess,
they stripped her naked and bound her;
these unchecked officials,
with their twisted viewpoint,
lashed her with thorns.

You could not bear to see the princess—
it would enrage you.
The people cry at the sight of her.

Who is responsible for enforcing this law?
Every sensible person is stunned senseless
at how pointless this is.

Even the birds, wild animals,
and flesh-eating beasts are weeping.
Gods and spirits moan and wail
from the formless realm.
The elements are disturbed,
the light of the sun and moon dimmed.
Quakes, floods, gales, hailstorms, and lightning rage.

Consider this: Who would create such karma?
King and Queen, no matter what you are thinking,
the entire realm is utterly stunned and disheartened.
Even your enemies think you've gone too far.

This is a princess of yours,
your own child.
Your officials and subjects see what's befallen her
and cannot believe it.

How do you feel about this?
At any rate, it would be better to banish her.
King, I beg you to say something!

The king responded,

Alas! Domestic official,
do you speak the truth?
Do not tell me lies;
be sure of your observations.
Talk we hear is half true, half false.
Bring the princess back into the palace
and ask if this tragedy took place.
As a favor to you, domestic official,
I could banish her to a jungle for a few years.

The king sent him to fulfill that order. Departing from the palace, this man addressed the princess and the state officials dispensing the punishment:

Pay heed! Princess, a pure, beaming glow adorns you.
An enthralling youth,
your very skin radiates light.
You dazzle with the hue of a dark-blue lotus,
as white-and-red lights swirl cloud-like around you.

The waft of your aroma resembles a water lily.
Your smile is a drop of smooth honey,
tinted the color of pomegranate.
Your hands and feet are like blossomed lotuses.

Your voice resembles a young swan on a lake.
An awakened hero of nondual compassion,
you reject causing anyone harm.
You are like light beaming from pure jewels.

In the past they were only able to admire you from afar,
and could never touch your soft, supple body.
Now you've been placed in the hands
of these vicious officials.

I witnessed you being forced to bow down
under their relentless, murderous noose
as they whipped your body with sharp thorns.
It disgusts me to think of that
and stops my very breath.

As for you officials,
you were greatly disturbed
when the princess rejected worldly conventions.
Is this the fruition of past karma
or merely fleeting misfortune?
No matter what you have in mind,
think very carefully about your every plan!
You have a high place among the subjects,
but the bonds of the royal family outrank you.

Put an end to your hostile feelings
toward this princess.
Release her ties,
return her clothing and jewelry to her,
and come inside the palace,
by order of the king!

The princess returned to the palace with the corrupt officials
to approach the king. Everyone outside assumed they had led her

in for an execution. They were distraught. Misery crushed their minds as they threw their bodies on the ground and wailed loudly.

The king, queen, officials, and subjects were all there in the palace. Each one exclaimed, "How could our beautiful princess bear this horror?" and then collapsed to the ground.

The king addressed her:

> Alas! Beautiful princess,
> you've suffered a great calamity.
> Bound, beaten, and miserable,
> yet still, you refuse to go.
> I am the one responsible for this.
>
> You are my own daughter
> with whom no one can compare,
> yet there can be no private deals concerning the king's law.
> For some years, you must go to a deserted place.
> We will meet after those years have passed.
> The justice officials will escort you
> a short distance into exile.

Once again, the princess appealed to her father:

> Pay heed! Great king,
> once you issue a command,
> what power do those officials have?
>
> As my parents, King and Queen,
> you were careless
> and I, your indispensable princess,
> was charged with this cruel law
> and placed directly in the hands
> of these unfit, vicious officials.

They whipped my lovely figure with thorns,
causing me unbearable terror and panic.
My body was awash with pus, blood, and bile—
the very sight of me made all your people cry.
Thinking of it breaks my heart.

King and Queen, you are my parents
and I will not defy your command.
Due to the major obscurations of my bad karma,
I will live my life in a deserted, haunted land.
Any rations of food, drink,
and clothing you offer me are fine.
If you give me nothing,
I will bear that as well.

We will not have the fortune
to meet again in this life.
May we meet in the next,
in Unsurpassable pure land

The state officials announced:

Pay heed! King, you are not thinking!
If she refuses to go where you send her,
she disregards your word.
What are you planning?
It's fitting to execute her,
but you can't bring yourself to do it!

Exiling her—
that's not an adequate punishment.
However, if you insist on this,
then she will be sent away
because we can't defy the king's law.

> Get on with it!
> Give her your gifts quickly.
> If she suffers for a long time,
> we will be satisfied.

Then the princess mounted an elephant. She was bound for exile north of the palace, in a place known as the Haunted Land of Ominous Jungles. Her parents offered her five hundred elephant loads of a large supply of food and drink. Five hundred ladies-in-waiting escorted her for the duration of the ten-day journey.

Once they reached a lower valley, called Medicinal Trees and Bushes, her escorts turned back toward the palace. Unable to bear leaving her, they looked in her direction, lamenting, "If we have to be apart from someone like you, beautiful princess, we must have made terrible aspirations!" The ladies-in-waiting wailed dreadfully as they returned home.

Among the escorts, one young lady, named Crystal Skull Earrings, of the Gar clan, was very wise and insightful. She and the princess had been intimate friends from a young age. Unable to fathom parting ways with her, she clutched at the princess's clothes and said:

> Your speech is as sweet
> as your body is blissful.
> Your altruistic mind-set
> entirely shapes your intentions.
> I care so much for you, my beloved.
>
> You have the youthful body of a sixteen-year-old,
> pale as the petals of a white lotus.
> Your soft skin is white with a rosy complexion.
> Your lotus fragrance wafts.
> Your hair is as deep blue as vine fruit.
> Your two eyes resemble new lotus buds.

The arch of your eyebrows
is like a mirage in space.
Your two ears resemble a flower with a thousand anthers.
The rounded tip of your nose is like a ruby.
Your luminous face laughs like a lotus abloom.

Your teeth are bright white like a flawless conch shell.
Your tongue is supple and delicate,
as if born from a lotus petal.
Your body feels pale and smooth,
tender and voluptuous.

The contour of your neck holds the victory banner
of the voice of Brahma.
Your delicate, supple waist resembles a flower stem.
Your feet move with a leisurely gait,
like a young swan.

You are a thousand-spoked wheel with a lotus border.
Latest to sleep and earliest to rise,
you are relaxed in your demeanor
and always a good friend.

Your mouth forms a radiant smile
and your eyes cast lovely sidelong glances.
Anywhere you are,
rainbow light encircles you an arm-span wide.

Attractive to behold,
your captivating, peaceful smile
beams like a ripe peach.
Resembling a lotus stem,
you are enchantingly beautiful,
youthful princess.

The sight of you captures my attention.
The thought of you moves me.
My enthrallment will be sated
when we can be together.

In the past until now,
our aspirations connected us.
Although I could see you,
I never had a chance to be with you.
Wishing for this,
we will be happy together for a long time.

Now we face obstacles
brought on by misfortune.
The vicious king and officials are terrible wrongdoers.
They exiled you,
an indispensable princess of the king's own flesh,
to an abandoned land
of savage, hostile gods and spirits.
That jungle is a dark place.
The screeches of its many birds will corrode your focus,
while having wild animals as companions will make
    you sad.

Princess, I dare not leave you in such a place!
We can go elsewhere,
to a site that is not the palace.
Wouldn't that be better?
Free from the high gaze of the king and officials,
we could be happy somewhere else.
I will stay with you, Princess.
Why shouldn't I?

The princess answered the young lady:

Your fresh youth is at its peak.
Your smiling face is like a lotus in bloom.
Your body is adorned
with the fivefold marks and signs of perfection.

Your luminous white complexion
resembles that of the deity Meaningful Lasso.
Your beautiful face is shaped like a wish-fulfilling jewel;
from any vantage point,
it bears the shape of a flower blossom.
You are like a medicinal shoot or lotus stem.

You speak gently, saying what's meaningful.
You are easygoing, restrained,
and dignified in your behavior.
You are like the rare udumbara flower.
You move gracefully as a bird.
The radiance of your bright smile enthralls me.
You are an incomparable young lady,
fully endowed with the marks and signs of physical
    perfection.

Although your yearning words are meant to be helpful,
I am incapable of defying my father's royal command.
Deceit cannot purify my past karma.
As for the hardship I face
in that deserted, Haunted Land of Ominous Jungles,
I will dedicate it to a better rebirth.

If I possess the mental fortitude for what I must do,
even exiled to an empty, deserted place,
I have few woes and regrets.
For some years, I will stay in that haunted land.
Until that time passes, young lady,

be happy in whatever way you choose
and I wish for us to swiftly meet again.

Once more, the young lady appealed to the princess:

We are connected through karma,
and my intentions led me to meet you,
beaming princess of exquisite youth.

You don't credit the words I say
and won't leave for a better place,
a comfortable and joyful land.

You insist on living
in that empty, uninhabitable jungle.
If that's the way it is,
I will follow you there.
Princess, do not send me away!
You tear out my heart, my lungs!
Away from you, I will fall apart.

I pray we may be together,
always and forever!
If I ever have to part with you,
smiling princess,
I will lose my mind!
My world will be bleak;
I will suffer like a mother
whose only child has died.
Since I feel this way,
I will stay with you in this empty land.

There is a pleasure grove
with an outspread green canopy,

where blue lotuses and water lilies grow.
The flowers' leaves and centers are laden with sap,
amid which bees hum and buzz.

The leaves and branches
of wish-fulfilling trees flutter in the breeze.
Aromatic trees smell fragrant as sweet honey.
Goddesses gather ambrosial flowers.
That place vividly enthralls me,
but without you, Princess,
it would be as flowers taken by frost.
So even this dreadful place doesn't matter:
I will stay wherever you are.
Allow me to be with you,
never apart in our yearning love.

The princess responded:

Young lady, although you speak the truth,
the suffering of one person is not meant for two.
This princess's past karma
led the king to reproach me
and the officials to punish me.
Though it's unbearable,
I have to shoulder the burden of my own faults.

Young lady, why go to this deserted land?
Return to the palace,
a source of happiness,
a golden cornucopia filled with fivefold wealth.

That is where your close friends
will exquisitely serve and revere you;
where together, the royal family, subjects, and court

gather good fortune.
Being with my ladies-in-waiting
will make your mind and world joyful.

Your longing for me enthralls you,
so much that you dare not leave.
Since you are so loving,
I offer you this jeweled ring from my finger,
young lady, in the spirit of affection.

I offer these elephant loads
of treasure vaults of gifts to my ladies-in-waiting
to relieve their sense of poverty.

I have no attachment to anyone or anything.
My mind in tune with the teachings
is my greatest wealth of joy.
Do not hold or cling to me!
I pray we will meet
in the expanse of enlightenment.

Dividing all the gifts carried on the elephants' backs, the princess offered them to her ladies-in-waiting without a second thought. After saying their parting words, their group returned to the palace.

The princess covered her body with leaves and went into the Haunted Land of Ominous Jungles. In a place called Lawa Shing Rongpuk, she gathered food, grasses, and fruit from white gooseberry trees and *Rosa sericea* trees. From the leaves of the *Rosa sericea*, she fashioned a seat and clothing. She also boiled its fruit to drink as tea.

Many peaceful animals, such as male and female deer, forest monkeys and apes, stayed with her. Even male and female carnivorous beasts kept her company as friends. Playful and joyous, they showed their good side. The princess fed them from the trees' bounty, and they lived together like a mother and her children.

In the leafy canopy above, the beautiful birds sang sweet songs, showing the princess their delight. All the trees' branches and leaves turned in her direction; the brooks and breezes flowed toward her. In the green mountain meadows, a bounty of exquisitely hued and deliciously scented flowers sprang up, unlike any that had grown before. A symphony of sweet sounds, with no discernible origin, emerged from the open sky. A large host of nonhuman gods and spirits gathered to honor and serve her, amid a continuous shower of various flowers.

Several months after the princess arrived in the Ominous Haunted Land, the king of Mighty Fortress heard she was living there. This saddened his son, the prince, who convened his sixty officials. Adorning himself with attractive jewelry and articles, he arranged for a grand, luxurious party. Then the prince requested their counsel.

"Important officials, use your considerable intelligence to cleverly devise a plan. That princess of the desert plains was exiled to the Haunted Land of Ominous Jungles, where she lives.

"Should we be diplomatic, asking the king and his officials for their princess? Do we mount a large army to abduct her? Would it be more cunning to carry jewelry and gifts to her, offer her many things, and once we take her attention, lure her to our palace? Discuss this, and decide which approach will accomplish our goal."

The officials had a meeting. "In the past, the Indian prince of Bhijara sought to marry this princess. Although her father, the king, and his officials made that prince a promise, she did not heed them. As a result, they exiled her to the Haunted Land.

"If we once again secure permission from her parents, but she doesn't wish to listen, it will be serious grounds for a dispute. Therefore, our prince should now assemble his court and a great deal of his wealth, then go see the princess where she lives. If he reasons with her insistently, she will listen and come with him."

Once they came to that agreement, they recounted their decision to the prince in great detail. Afterward, the prince and sixty officials gathered a great many items from their treasure vault of wealth. They presented these gifts to the princess's parents, as well as to the princes and their wives, in order to request the marriage.

The king, officials, and subjects responded:

> The princess is utterly beautiful and enthralling,
> an excellent match to become your prince's wife.
> Indispensable to us,
> we give her to you as a king's queen.
>
> That said, she does not heed our counsel.
> The prince can announce this,
> but she won't listen to anyone.
> We promise to give her to you.
> Take the princess to your palace.

Having received their clear answer, the prince assembled five hundred young men. He had five hundred elephants loaded with his goods, including supplies of food and drink. They left and quickly drew close to the Haunted Land of Ominous Jungles.

Their arrival enraged that haunted land's tigers, bears, brown bears, and other carnivorous beasts. Snarling in distress, they blocked the road so no one could pass. Blizzards and gales raged, halting passage through the forests. At this point, trees surrounded the prince's entourage and his many possessions. They stayed under the cover of branches and leaves.

Eventually, the prince and his entourage ventured onward. Having reached the jungle, they couldn't find where the princess lived and lost heart. At daybreak one morning, a large band of apes and monkeys appeared. Carrying fruit and smiling joyfully, they headed toward the upper part of the valley.

When the prince, his officials, and court followed them, they discovered a clearing in a grove of lotus flowers. This held a large green meadow of flowers, grasses, and fruit trees. A canopy of *Rosa sericea* trees swayed in the breeze, amid the soft murmur of a stream. Myriads of beautiful birds perched in the branches, singing vivid songs. In this expansive valley, the earth was soft and verdant; a strong breeze circulated many sweet aromas of delicious foods.

At the base of a round *Rosa sericea* tree, the princess rested in the shade of its leaves and branches. She was exquisite to behold. Beautiful and enthralling, her complexion was as clear and white as a lotus. Young male and female monkeys, apes, birds, and other wild animals were gathered all around her, smiling in joyful delight. They continued to frolic playfully as the prince approached. Drawing near, as soon as their eyes met, he gazed at the princess and spoke:

> The sight of you enthralls me,
> joyfully smiling young lady.
> Looking at you moves me.
> Your words inspired my certainty.
>
> You are always on my mind:
> these thoughts make ordinary life gloomy.
> Never forgetting you,
> you are ever more vivid in my imagination.
> Sick at heart, I forgot about food and clothing.
>
> Thinking of you, young lady,
> I can't focus my attention elsewhere,
> even as my body's channels, energies,
> and essence blaze with joyful bliss.
>
> When I think of you,
> that imprint stays on my mind.
> Now that I hear your words,
> it's like a dream or illusion.

Now that I see you,
these impressions flood my mind.

Now my resolve, my thrall, my desire are sated.
Now that I see your face,
won't you speak to me?

The princess looked at the prince and replied:

You are young and handsome
like a lotus flower.
The sound of your sweet, pure words
has the sheen of cleverness,
and you are attractive to look at from this close.

Yet no matter what you say,
this is a deserted, empty land of gods and spirits:
there is no human man here like you.
You are a magic trick of gods and spirits,
a cunning way to fool me.

I am a low-class woman
living in a deserted, empty land.
We've met, but I don't know what your words mean.
No matter what you say, young man,
you should return home.
This is a haunted land;
there is nothing here for people.

A destitute woman with apes and birds as friends,
I am like a child of wild animals.
Avoid the company of someone so unclean.
Young man, we should remain apart.

The prince told the princess:

Your youth is enthralling,
your body delightful,
and your smile demure.
You are as voluptuous as a white swan,
shapely like a flower.

Your aroma is sweet-smelling
and you have a dignified manner.
Your melodious speech enchants me
beyond any other.

Unforgettable princess,
thinking of you inspired me.
You, Princess, were on this young man's mind,
and I journeyed here quickly from Mighty Fortress.
I made a long voyage, driven by love,
risking my life to face a pack of carnivorous beasts,
crossing over passes and valleys
to arrive here before you.

I am a person, a man,
not a magic trick of the spirits.
I am free from every impurity
and have a medicinal fragrance,
like flower nectar in a pleasure garden.

Princess, why can't we be together?
Thinking of you,
I speak words from the heart.
Driven by that love,
I wanted to rush here and meet you.

Young lady, like a lotus flower abloom
with your bright, laughing smile,
I traveled far. Become my wife!

Abandon this empty, uninhabitable, haunted land
and come to my opulent palace.
Young lady, be there with me,
and you can do as you please.

She answered:

Young man, your words are meant to help me,
yet this princess will not go elsewhere.
Foolish, undependable people
exiled me from the palace.
They didn't appreciate me
and delivered me to this deserted land.

You are a king's son from a noble line,
yet as you think of matrimony,
I delight in having wild animals as friends.

Your palace is a site of great wealth,
while my site of meditative stability
is a deserted valley, empty and isolated.
As for your court, subjects, and others,
no matter how lofty they are,
my basic nature is my companion;
apes and monkeys are my court.

Your golden, turquoise jewelry
and articles have a noble sheen,
but my wearing leaves causes little harm.
Your consuming meat and alcohol
is delicious in your mouth,
while my eating fruit
ripens into bliss and heat in my body.

You travel swiftly by horse,
as I harness my circulating energy
to reach the level of bliss.

Your family is important
and you have your father's solid name,
while I am an excellent adept who practices the teachings
as spiritual attainment keeps me company.

No matter how noble your clan,
how lofty your royal line,
my mind's blissful basic nature
is comfortable in a humble position.

Worldly activities do not thrill me.
Young man, you too should enjoy the wealth
of the sacred teachings.

The prince responded:

Youthful princess, your beauty enthralls me.
Lovingly heed these words I speak to you.

By all means, if you insist on practicing,
there will be no barriers
to your efforts in my palace.
The kingdom's leaders are devoted,
and so wish to honor you.
The subjects, servants, and court have equanimity,
so they wish to protect and serve you.

As much as their hands are able,
they wish to give you food and drink.
As much as their bodies are able,

they wish to revere you with offerings.
As much as their voices are able,
they wish to give you supportive advice.
As much as their minds are able,
they wish to be altruistic and compassionate.

When you understand this,
you can practice as you like!
I speak with your well-being in mind.
Captivating lady,
if you do not come to the palace,
it plants a seed of wrongdoing
far greater than any basis for good.
I'm speaking from the heart,
so won't you listen to me?

Once again, the princess addressed him:

Prince, though you speak well,
motivated by love,
even if it were best to practice in your palace,
I will not do that.
Young man, heed my well-chosen words.

On the ocean lies a bright, joyous place,
a land of desirable jewels,
faultless and free from attachment.

Lush fields and meadows
hold flowers and medicinal plants
brimming with aromatic pure nectar
and ambrosial sweet scents,
where swarms of bees flit about in delight.

Intelligent birds sing melodious songs,
their beating wings gently stirring the air.
Sparkling water flows pure and unpolluted
as a shimmering rain of flowers fills the sky.

That pleasure garden
is a floral, green space.
Young man, if we were together
in that gorgeous place,
surrounded by ambrosial flowers,
being in love would seem to sate our desire.

Nevertheless, just to see that spectacle in our minds
doesn't mean finding happiness there.
It would be the cause of delusion.
So I will live in this empty valley
with no people, no attachment, no clinging.

Young prince, do not resent this princess.
We will soon meet again,
so return to your palace.
I come from a bad family,
and marrying me will not make you happy.
Your family line is noble just as it is.

When you stay in your palace,
your subjects and court are content.
Live with faith, according to the teachings,
and rule your kingdom based on spiritual ideals.

Why won't you listen to these words?
My heartfelt advice is kind and helpful.

The prince implored:

> Beautiful princess, your words are very kind
> and this youth holds them in high regard.
>
> If I can't fulfill my wish
> through the power of happiness,
> then I'm an ignorant fool
> who pretended to be wise.
>
> Youthful lady, if it's not worthwhile to marry me,
> anything I say is like water running over rocks.
> Now listen to me and keep this in mind, my beauty.
>
> You've settled in a garden valley
> in this empty snow mountain range;
> the echo on its mud and slate is disheartening.
>
> Here stands a brambly forest clearing
> surrounded by various trees with outspread leaves.
> The hearts of aromatic flowers
> hold colorful pollen the bees collect.
> Under a cool canopy,
> small forest birds warble tunes
> amid the melodious symphony of songbirds.
>
> Cuckoos and parrots gather dew-laden fruit
> over the murmur of a pure, unpolluted spring.
> Young monkeys, apes, deer, and birds
> live among the sandalwood and *Rosa sericea* trees.
>
> This empty, deserted land makes me sad.
> As a long-term home
> to cultivate meditation and stability,
> this is not the place for you, beautiful lady.

Enthralling princess—
come be my queen in the palace!
You will have time to consider
these peaceful, joyous words I speak.
Driven by my affection,
I don't dare leave you.

Come with me to the palace.
Stop being so bold
and speaking so stubbornly.
Youthful lady, you will be like a flower in the palace
and I, too, will be a pure cool breeze of sweet nectar.

If even now, you refuse to join me
so we can be together forever,
I will not make obstacles
to your positive activities.
Is this the case?
Then I make haste to leave.

Saying this, he gazed longingly at the princess. Tears filling his eyes, he gasped until the breath caught in his chest and sobbed miserably.

Two officials from the prince's court witnessed their exchange. Greatly saddened, they discussed the matter. "If the princess refuses to come to the palace, our prince will be devastated. He will surely die! So we have to take her to the palace by force, immediately. That's the right thing to do." The two officials seized her by both arms, saying,

Joined by the power of aspirations,
you've been told to marry him.
Like a flower and its nectar,
you two, Prince and Princess,
will be the best couple,

together forever.
We ask you to come with us to the palace,
where you will be happy as can be.

The officials hurriedly dragged the princess to the passageway leading out of the valley. This distressed all the creatures there, including the monkeys, apes, birds, and deer. They screamed and cried. Some fainted, their bodies going stiff. Some collapsed, stunned. Some followed after her. In that area, all the blossoms closed up, every tree limb cracked, and the green of the valley faded. Then the princess addressed the officials:

Karma arranged for you both to be officials—
you have the strength of a savage man,
the malice of a thief,
and you fail as caring allies of the spiritual teachings—
you vicious officials are low-class!

When you harm others,
it will return to you.
That creates suffering
for this life and the next,
so do not assault me.
Allow me to stay in this deserted land.

Saying that, she held on to a tree. Driving her hands and feet into earth and rock, she wept and screamed.
The two officials lashed her with a whip of thorns as they spoke:

Beautiful, enchanting lady,
you are a princess,
so you speak well,
yet you refuse to heed the prince.
If you will not come to the palace,

no clever words will change this.
We travel there in haste.

The officials quickly led her across passes and valleys. Along the way, they encountered the rest of the entourage they had left behind. The moment they met the princess, everyone praised her in unison:

Your superb attributes and bright smile enthrall us;
your young body is in the bloom of youth.

Wondrous in these four ways,
you are pale in color and voluptuous,
your body is fragrant,
your voice is clear,
and your manner is dignified.

Like the blossom of a crabapple tree,
you are not subject to the flaws of attachment.

Seeing you dispels our sense of poverty and misery.
Hearing you brings bliss to our minds.
Remembering the sight of you satiates us.

We officials and subjects are all low-class.
How kind of you to be our prince's queen!
How wondrous of you to live in our palace!

Once they dressed her in numerous garments and adorned her with jewelry, they bound her four limbs with chains. She was placed on an elephant's back, while the officials and subjects rode excellent horses. Surrounding the princess, they rushed through valleys and passes toward the palace.

One evening, they made camp in a clearing of trees only a day's journey from the palace of Mighty Fortress. All the other ladies, officials, and subjects came from there to escort them, arriving clad in their best finery. The court, lords, and subjects were overjoyed to welcome a princess like this to become their prince's queen. They celebrated with a great feast of meat and alcohol. Feeling happy, they went off to sleep.

As for the officials and young men originally dispatched to invite her, they thought, "We went a long way to take this princess. Our officials and subjects have come to welcome her. We are happy with our success." Eating meat and drinking alcohol, everyone became intoxicated. Relaxed, they fell asleep.

The prince also considered this. "I went a great distance to invite the princess; my officials and subjects are fully satisfied. We are very close to reaching the palace. How wonderful! I am powerful enough to marry a princess as enchanting as this one. I've succeeded!" Then he went to his brocade tent and fell asleep.

That night passed. At daybreak, the princess's mind was utterly clear. She thought, "If I look at myself and really reflect on who I am, I took a low birth, with the bad karma of a body like my own. My mind is dull, my knowledge is trivial, and I've experienced so much misfortune. Although I think of spiritual practice, I have no agency to pursue it. Why must all of this land on me? I am defeated. Lamas and dakinis, do you have any compassion? Is it possible that just one thing could happen according to my wishes?"

Lamenting and wailing, she made this supplication:

> Hri! Primordial triumphant buddha of nondual
>   compassion,
> loving protector, do your eyes see me or not?
> I'm someone who lacks awareness and has terrible karma,
> wandering in the darkness of the round of rebirth.
>
> Does the chronic disease of the three poisons grip me
>   or not?
> Will you free me from this fearsome ravine or not?

Will I face the misfortune of my bad karma or not?
I beseech you to grant this unsheltered woman a sanctuary!

Loving protector, be generous with your nondual
    compassion.
The round of rebirth is devoid of awareness.
Lead me out of here
and swiftly place me in supreme bliss!

She supplicated with a fine voice, her mind full of yearning. At
that moment, a white-colored man appeared. His hair was knotted
around a crystal at the crown of his head. Holding a turquoise vase,
he spoke to her:

You have previous good karma and fortune.
Your mind favors positive acts.
You are a woman with the utmost faith.
Ground your thoughts and actions within mindfulness.
Faith is an ally that carries you along the path.
Compassion and emptiness are indivisibly united.
The universe and all it holds are like a dream or illusion.
Insubstantial mind itself dissolves into space.
Do not be sad; this is your share of spiritual attainment.
Meditate on misfortune arising as your ally.

The princess thought, "This man does not seem like a human. Is
he the emanation of a buddha? How amazing!"

She said to him, "I have never seen a man like you before. You are
not a human being. Which pure land did you come from? What sort
of being are you? What is your name? What are you doing here?"

In response to her questions, he replied, "I've come from the land
of Oddiyana, known as the site of an ocean of dakinis. The family I belong to is Buddha Ever-Excellent. My name is Lotus-Born.
I have disciples in India, spread out from east to west. What is my
aim? I've come to accompany you. Three years have passed since

I came to this land of the Tibetan people, at a place called Samyé Chimpu. You never saw me?"

The princess implored, "If you are the Lotus-Born King of Oddiyana, and you would be my companion in spiritual practice as you hold me with your compassion, then isn't this the right thing for me to do? Is there some way you can free me from the prison of these iron chains?"

Lotus-Born of Oddiyana told her, "If you want to practice, Princess, I will accompany you. Slip this jeweled band on the ring finger of your left hand. Meditate on me in the form of an adept at the crown of your head. Follow me wherever I go, harboring no doubts. The royal family, court, and subjects will not see us."

When the princess placed his band on her ring finger, the iron chains binding her four limbs fell away. She regained her physical vitality. Then, following Lotus-Born of Oddiyana, they reached the place known as Samyé Chimpu in an instant.

When the two of them arrived there, the prince woke up. He looked for the princess but couldn't find her. In the open sky, he saw a male and female couple, a hero and a dakini, flying in the direction of India. The officials he had originally dispatched saw a black raptor carrying a small, brown pigeon in its mouth. It flew through the sky toward India. All those in the welcome party saw a vajra and bell falling in the direction of Samyé.

The prince and everyone in his court searched the clearing for the princess. Failing to find her, the prince felt angry and dejected. All the officials looked at their prince and cried loudly. The court and subjects fainted and collapsed.

Once everyone regained their wits, they spoke in unison. "That troublemaker princess! Either she escaped to her father, or the Indian prince of Bhijara abducted her. Whatever the case, it is due to previous karma. We should all return to our palace." Agreeing on this, each person went home.

At the palace of the princess's family, known as Draktsal Ger, her father, the king, his officials, royal family, court, and subjects heard many rumors flying back and forth. Understanding that the king of Mighty Fortress had enthroned her, they were overjoyed and sent people to that palace.

As for the prince of Mighty Fortress, he asked, "I'm wondering if the princess's father abducted her or not? In order to have her, I gave gifts to that king and his officials, which they accepted. I'm furious! If that's the case, they are obligated to return the princess to me."

He dispatched five hundred swift horses to deliver this message. As they raced along the road, that group encountered the two people sent from the princess's family's palace of Tsalukar. They told them how the princess had fled and couldn't be found. The groups traded hateful accusations and everyone became furious. Their faces darkened; each group returned to their own palace.

At Tsalukar, her father, the king, mounted a large army. Outraged, he roared, "We are going to destroy the royal family, officials, and subjects of Mighty Fortress!"

Lotus-Born of Oddiyana knew the situation would cause many murders and create bad karma. Looking at this with great compassion, he emanated two princesses, both women of superb qualities.

One princess appeared at Tsalukar, to the delight of all the royal family, officials, and court. That area was once again an auspicious place where the spiritual teachings flourished.

The other princess appeared at Mighty Fortress, delighting their royal family, officials, and subjects. This area also became auspicious once more, and the spiritual teachings prevailed for a long time.

Then in the place called Samyé Chimpu, which is equal to India's Cool Grove charnel ground, the princess and Lotus-Born of Oddiyana lived and practiced together, without a moment's separation.

That concludes the first chapter, in which I, the princess, explain how I was born.

Samaya
Gya Gya Gya
Da-yik x9

2: The Princess's Voyages
to the Land of Oddiyana

The princess stood before Guru Rinpoche of Oddiyana. As an offering, she took the turquoise gemstone, called Blazing Light Jewel, from the crown of her head and placed it on a mirror of white silver. She beseeched him:

> Supreme Adamantine Master,
> I have taken this low birth as a woman,
> yet I hold myself in high regard.
>
> I don't have much goodness and wisdom,
> though what little I did cultivate in the past
> led to my rebirth as the daughter of a cruel king.
>
> I don't have much goodness and wisdom,
> yet I did manage to meet a lama like you,
> who embodies the buddhas
> of the past, present, and future.
>
> Moreover,
> since we women have these bodies,
> my knowledge is trivial
> and my character spoiled.
>
> As someone at a major disadvantage,
> who lacks faith and courage,

I implore you to give me instructions
in few words with great meaning,
so that I might swiftly attain enlightenment.

Guru Rinpoche replied:

Attractive princess, listen well.
Due to your birth in a woman's body
and scarce cultivation of goodness and wisdom,
swift enlightenment will be a challenge.

Birth as a male leper
or as a woman with courage—
these are both positive,
but each has a flaw.
However, if you have faith and perseverance,
there is a chance you will attain enlightenment.

Princess, give up your plans for this life!
Without holding anything back,
dedicate your body and life force
to cultivate your experience
of these ultimate instructions for meditation.

This charnel ground of Samyé Chimpu
is a site where dakinis and furies visibly gather.
Stay here in retreat for twelve years
and apply these meditation instructions.

As for me, I leave for India soon,
but will quickly return to Tibet.
During that time, Princess,
gain accomplishment!

He spoke emphatically, then gave her the cycle of great perfection teachings for transformation from an ordinary state to a body free of defilements. After that, he flew toward India with the four tribes of dakinis.

"At Samyé Chimpu charnel ground, I, the princess, lived in Secret Wisdom Cave. I fashioned a meditation seat from grasses found in the charnel ground. To sustain my meditation practice, I gathered nutritious fruits; to slake my thirst, I drank water. Without a second thought, I committed my body and life to practice, and took an oath not to turn back."

One month later, a white-colored woman appeared at daybreak before the entrance of her retreat hut. She knocked on the door with a crystal staff; the princess told her to open it. The woman did, looked inside, and asked, "What are you doing, Princess?"

"I am cultivating meditative concentration."

"As you do this, do you have faith?"

"Yes, I have faith when I meditate."

"You may have faith, but it is not true faith. In my country, we have true faith."

The princess considered this. "I have seen an actual buddha in Guru Rinpoche of Oddiyana himself, and no faith is greater than this." This thought bolstered her self-assurance.

The woman knew what was in her mind and replied, "Follow me, Princess. I will show you authentic faith."

She led her by the hand and they arrived in a country where the land was white. A palace stood there, with tiered overhangs ornamented in pearl, turquoise, and gold. On its roof, banners fluttered around a lovely parasol that had a lattice of dangling bells. A canopy of rainbows and light enfolded the palace.

Many wealthy villages stretched around its perimeter. Forests of lotuses and sandalwood trees grew there, from which wafted many aromas of sweet fruits and pleasant fragrances. Large medicinal trees and bright flowers filled a massive pleasure garden.

Having landed there in that amazing place, they spent the day sightseeing among the marvels. They visited a large square crowded with people, amid which stood an enormous golden throne. It had turquoise columns, a canopy of five-colored gemstones, and a lotus seat placed under a sun and moon. A grandiose king sat there, white in color. He was handsome and youthful, his body lavishly adorned.

Everyone gathered in the square looked humbly toward the king as they did forceful prostrations with their bodies. Removing their jewelry, they offered it to him. As gifts, the parents presented their sons and daughters; children offered both their mother and father. Those most skilled in respectful service freely lavished the king with wealth and jewels.

The princess thought, "This is not a king who embodies the spiritual teachings. These people's humble respect is pointless. In this context, making offerings of jewels and wealth without a second thought will not gain them any stores of goodness. What are these people doing?"

She asked her companion, "What is the name of this place? What do they call this palace? What is that king's name? What are the people of this town doing?"

The woman replied, "Princess, listen to me! This land is called Lotus Array. This palace is known as Center of Great Bliss. The king's name is Youthful Meditative State. These townsfolk have humble faith in this king, so they make offerings to please him."

The princess demanded, "Does this king even have spiritual teachings to give? When these people make offerings, what stores of goodness will they gain? Isn't he an ordinary human king, a powerful person? Doesn't he aggressively collect their wealth and jewels?"

The woman told her, "You have no faith, Princess. Of course he's a king who embodies the spiritual teachings! These townsfolk have faith, so they see him as such. To please the king, they would give their lives without hesitation. If your intentions are pure, this king's nondual compassion is completely unbiased."

Another day, a crowd gathered in the square. There, the king was killing many people. He ate their flesh, drank their blood, chewed their bones, and wore their flayed skins. Those townsfolk gazed upon the king and supplicated him with humble respect.

The princess asked her companion, "How can the people of this town be filled with humble respect for this king even as he murders them?"

She replied, "These townsfolk regard the king's actions as good, no matter what he does."

Another day, a crowd gathered in the square. There, the king proclaimed in a booming voice, "All these rocks are food! Eat them!" Even though the rocks broke the teeth in their mouths, everyone there enthusiastically ate them with great courage.

The princess asked, "Why are the people of this town eating these rocks even as their teeth shatter?"

"You have no faith, Princess. No matter what the king says, these townsfolk understand it to be true."

Another day, a crowd gathered in the square. There, the king gave a dram of poison to each person and said, "Drink this quickly!" They courageously ingested the poison, although it caused ruptures in their bodies until they collapsed.

The princess asked her companion, "Why are the people of this town drinking poison even as it causes them to faint and collapse?"

"Listen to me, Princess. These townsfolk are willing to do anything the king asks of them."

Another day, a crowd gathered in the square. The king told them, "This morning at daybreak, gather a mass of riches, like a rain of flowers. Do this to please me." The wealthy people gave him golden horses adorned with turquoise ornaments, jeweled treasure vaults, and turquoise elephants loaded with distilled sweet nectar. Every father, mother, and child donned stunning jewelry in order to offer their body, speech, and mind to the king. The poor people wrapped their naked bodies in rags taken from the charnel ground. Making a pyre of sandalwood, they burned themselves as offerings to him.

The princess asked her companion, "Why are the people of this town taking their jewels, wealth, and even their own lives, and offering everything, without hesitation, to this king?"

The woman replied, "Listen to me, Princess. These townsfolk are willing to offer as much as they have to the king."

She took the princess by the hand and led her before him. "Great king, bless this princess to quickly liberate her from the lower realms."

The king responded, "Princess, do you have authentic faith or not? If you have faith, I can give you my blessing."

"I do have authentic faith," she answered.

He said, "I know whatever your mind holds, Princess. That faith of yours is not authentic. You view your lama and me, the king, as separate. This is authentic faith:

> Everything I do, you see as excellent.
> Everything I say, you take to be true.
> Everything I give you, you are ready to consume.
> Everything I ask of you, you are willing to do.
> Everything you possess, you gladly offer.

You have to be like the people of this town."

She considered this. "My own faith is so fickle. I'm ashamed! How incredible that all the people of this town, young and old, have authentic faith. I'm certain that this king possesses an enlightened lineage. I must ask for meditation instructions to swiftly attain enlightenment."

Thinking of this, she offered three prostrations. At that point, the king and his followers inside the palace flew into the sky on five-colored horses of light.

Her companion spoke, insisting, "Listen to me, Princess. Your faith didn't measure up, so you cannot meet the king. Pay attention to that!"

Once again, the woman took her by the hand, saying, "There's a place even more amazing over there!" They arrived in a bright, yellow valley. At the center of that area rose a multistory palace with golden eaves. On its roof stood an open parasol with a lattice of pearls, jewels, and small bells. Numerous villages and iron fences surrounded that lovely place.

To the south lay a pool glowing with five-colored lights and ringed by bright, sweetly aromatic flowers. Its edges were crowded with beautiful young women and men. They bathed themselves and feasted on food and drink.

Among that group, one especially vibrant young woman stood out. With her hands, she constantly made offerings. With her unwavering voice, she made supplications to the awareness-holder lamas. Looking at wretched beings stricken by exhaustion and poverty, tears flowed like blood from her eyes. She ran in circles around the pool completely naked, without a stitch of clothing on her body.

Upon seeing this girl, the princess asked her companion, "Here in this town, what are all these men and women doing crowded around the pool's edge? In particular, why is this naked young woman moving so quickly and acting so harried?"

The woman answered, "Take stock of what you're seeing, Princess. Understand that the men and women around this pool are washing away their impurities—they are cleansing physical, verbal, and mental defilements.

"As for this naked, rushing woman, recalling death and impermanence makes her worried and fearful that her hands aren't quick enough, and she won't have time to make offerings.

"Why does she repeatedly supplicate with her voice? Only qualified lamas can provide refuge from the three lower realms; she is worried and fearful that she won't have time to supplicate the lamas.

"Why does she look at wretched beings and cry tears like blood? She is worried that she, too, will be reborn as one of them.

"Why does she race around the pool? This luminous pool is a wellspring of qualities. She circles the pool because she is fearful that there isn't enough time to reach spiritual attainment.

"Why is she stark naked? She is cultivating stores of goodness.

Thinking that death will come if she pauses to dress herself, she is fearful that she won't have time for her cultivations."

Then the princess asked her companion, "What does this palace hold?"

"In this palace we'll find many examples of liberation. Let's go see."

They entered and saw a mound of gold and turquoise at the center of a large courtyard. Nearby, an attractive and handsome man sat on a tiered throne of jewels. A crowd of imbeciles, with large bodies and very thin throats, surrounded him. That lavishly adorned young king severed his own left leg and tossed it to those wretched people. Occasionally, he took gold and turquoise from the pile and offered it for them to enjoy. Sometimes he would settle his gaze and rest in evenness. Catching sight of the princess and her companion, he spoke to them.

"What are you two doing here? Do you have time to spare in this life? Are you human women or not? Are you immune to birth and death?"

The princess answered, "I am a human woman, subject to birth and death. I know I have no time to spare in this life. As for why we're here, I came to see you, the king of this palace."

He shouted at them, "If you know you don't have time to spare in this life, how have you found time to come to this palace and see me? How shameful! What is there to see here, looking at me? Don't you know that death will come?

"For my part, I, the king, have no idea when death arrives, so I'm in a panic! It's been a long while since I took the time to eat or drink. Worried that I wouldn't have time to hand out gifts from my treasure vault of jewels, I had to sever a leg from my body to give away. Worried that I wouldn't even have time to offer my own flesh, I had to look at my mind and settle in evenness to prepare for death.

"Furthermore, I don't have time to talk with you two. I don't know when I will die, so stop getting in my way. Leave this palace!"

Her companion said, "As things stand, Princess, you will not gain freedom. Look at the woman by that pool and the king in this palace. You spend your life in constant laziness; you have no time for enlightenment."

Utterly disheartened by her own lack of diligence, the princess fainted and collapsed. When she revived and regained her wits, she looked at the king. He melted into light and she saw him attain complete, manifest enlightenment.

The women left the palace. At the poolside, that harried, naked young lady held a bell and vajra in her hands. Seated on rays of light, she flew into space. They watched her attain complete, manifest enlightenment as well.

"Let's go," the princess's companion said. They went to a blue-green land that held a sea with grassy banks. A grove of flowers grew there. At its center rose a small, jeweled mountain surrounded by towns. Four large rivers flowed down the mountain's four sides, between which grew orchards of aromatic fruits. A cluster of jewels crowned its summit. It was appealing from any vantage point.

On the mountain's south side stood a town built from blue bricks and surrounded by a gold fence. At its center rose a palace with an open turquoise parasol on its roof. This palace reached nearly twelve miles in height and twenty-one miles across.

When they approached it, two large women blocked the door so no one could enter. They asked the princess and her companion, "You two—where are you going and what are you doing?" Each large woman carried a massive iron vase and held a human corpse on her lap. Sneering, they bit down on their lower lips and watched with a piercing gaze.

The princess replied, "We come from a place called Chimpu charnel ground. We are going to see what marvels the castle holds, so don't block the way. Let us go as we please."

The pair of large women replied, "If you two enter the castle, are you willing to carry heavy loads? Can you handle this?"

The massive vase they carried was filled with one hundred corpses. The princess tried to hoist it onto her back and exclaimed, "Both of us can't lift something like this! Is there another way to enter the palace? Anyhow, why should we carry it?"

The large women insisted, "If you do not shoulder this load, there is no way to enter the palace. This iron vase is the vessel by which you will receive spiritual attainment. As for the corpses inside, they are what you will use to request it; offer them as a ritual feast." With that, the pair went inside, shutting the outer gateway tightly so no one could enter.

The princess asked her companion, "Is there another way in?"

"There is. Let's go visit the town square," she replied.

When they arrived, they saw a crowd of people carrying gold bars the same size as their bodies. Shaking and staggering, the joints of their arms and legs cracked. Everyone wept and moaned loudly.

The princess asked them, "Even as your bones break, you still carry these gold bars. Why are you doing this?"

The group answered, "After we offer these to the king and queen in the palace, we can claim the reward we crave."

"What is this reward you desire so much?" she asked.

"We want today's ration of food."

"Do you have to carry a burden like this in return for today's meal?"

"If we don't, the king and queen will be upset and won't offer us what we want."

The princess considered this. "Each day, driven by hunger and thirst, all those people are bravely willing to do what they must. If I compare myself to them, I'm disheartened by my own lack of courage in relation to spiritual practice."

She returned to the palace door with her companion, who shouted, "Great adept, open this door!" A large woman, different from the previous ones, appeared. Tall and dark blue in color, naked and radiant, she had red eyes and excellent hair. This time, she opened the door.

They entered and found themselves on the ground floor of the palace, where a crowd of women had gathered. Among them, the large ones ate flesh and drank blood. The small ones peeled the skin from the soles of their feet and ate their own flesh.

Alarmed, the princess asked her companion, "Why are these women acting this way?"

"This is the land of dakinis and furies. The chiefs among them eat flesh and drink blood. They are the most powerful ones. Their servants consume their own flesh and blood in the hopes of ascending to the ranks of chief. Do you understand?"

The princess thought, "For all their courage, they hope for such a small reward. Compared to them, someone like me is appalling! I don't even keep the spiritual teachings in mind; that is the worst fault."

They ascended to the palace's middle level, where a golden turquoise-inlaid throne stood on four jeweled legs. A great, resplendent king sat there, his immense figure dark blue in color. He wore his hair in a knot atop his head, skins on his body, and bones across his shoulders. He sat amid dazzling light, holding a sun and moon as his three eyes delivered a piercing gaze.

Before him stood the queen, a young woman with three eyes. A red lotus with five petals emerged from her heart. The princess and her companion understood its blessings to be far greater than any others.

The king told the queen, "Give a pill to those dakinis and furies." Each one swallowed it, melted into light, and ascended into space.

The princess saw this and thought, "If I have that pill, I won't need spiritual practice. This is enlightenment itself! I have to request one as well."

"Please give me a pill," she asked the queen, who replied, "You were unwilling to carry that iron vase filled with one hundred human corpses. Therefore, I can't offer you a pill. Only those with courage can receive it." This left the princess disappointed and ashamed.

After that, she and her companion ascended to the palace's upper level. On the ceiling, victory banners made of human skins were raised in the four directions. Four hearts blazed radiantly in the four upper corners. The supporting beams were crafted from dried skulls. Outwardly, the building appeared as a jeweled palace, while inwardly its decorations were typical of a charnel ground. Everything appeared warm and resplendent.

A large crowd of women had gathered there. When they saw the princess's companion, they all prostrated to her and touched her feet. Delighted and overjoyed, they cried, "Our chief, Lives in Peace, has come back from her tour of the Tibetan people's charnel grounds."

"This is my home," said her companion. "Now return to your own place, where there is a bounty of amazing spiritual attainment to gain." Saying that, she made a show of pointing to the palace door.

"I can't go there and manage on my own! Won't you come along?" the princess pleaded.

"I don't have time to go with you. I have to stay here and protect the lives of these adepts who uphold their tantric bonds. Leave here bravely. Before, your fault was that you lacked courage. Isn't that why you didn't receive an uncontaminated pill? Go and don't doubt yourself!"

After that, the princess left through the palace's gate and traveled west. The land she found was wide, vast, and red in color. A dazzling five-colored canopy of light enfolded it. Every drop of water was rushing blood; bones covered every inch of land; all the mountain peaks blazed with fire amid a deluge of suns and moons raining down.

A large town stood there, built from five kinds of jewels. In its midst rose five distinctive, grand palaces. One stood in the middle, surrounded by four others in the cardinal directions. The eastern palace was bright white; the southern, brilliant yellow; the western, lustrous red; and the northern, splendid green. The central palace glowed radiantly with all five colors. In height and breadth, they extended as far as the eye could see. Jewels and dangling bells adorned their walls; their roofs were beautified with parasols, victory banners, and wheels.

A grove of lotuses and sandalwood trees encircled the palaces.

Five kinds of flowers blanketed the earth. A vajra fence, with four immense gates in each direction, surrounded everything. All the residents had skin of those same colors; they glowed with light. Some were utterly terrifying and repeatedly roared angry words. Others were enchantingly lovely.

The princess approached the eastern gate. A number of tall, dark-blue women with large, black eyes demanded, "What are you doing here? Go away!" They seized her hands, then lifted her up and threw her down. Sharp pains made the princess lose her bearings and faint.

As she regained her senses, the women bellowed with uproarious laughter and pushed her away. The princess said, "I come from a site called Samyé Chimpu charnel ground. This palace is said to be a place to visit in order to gain spiritual attainment. That's what I, too, seek and that's why I came here."

"Who told you that about this place?" asked one woman.

"In the land of Tibet there lives a supreme adept known as Lotus-Born of Oddiyana. He gave me this command: 'Stay in this charnel ground and meditate for twelve years.' While living and practicing there, a white-colored woman appeared. She led me away, saying, 'You're going to a pure land,' and I was powerless to resist."

One of the women adepts at the gate grabbed her hand and said, "I could allow you to enter, but what sort of gift can you offer me?"

The princess replied, "I want to give you something. I have no food or anything of value to offer, but if it pleases you, you can have the flesh from my limbs."

"I don't want your flesh. You have to kill a mother tigress and her cub in the jungle, then give me that flesh."

The princess considered this. "If I go into the jungle to kill a mother tigress, I'll pay a heavy price for my wrongdoing. Besides not gaining the spiritual attainment, I'll have that bad karma to bear. Since I don't have any tigress flesh to offer them, these gate-guardian adepts will continue to block the way and I can't enter the palace. Whatever I do, it seems like I won't reach what I came for."

Feeling disheartened and regretful, she mulled this over day and night. Then she thought, "If I venture into the jungle, perhaps I can find a dead tigress and cub."

The princess entered the jungle full of lotuses and sandalwood trees. Searching far and wide, she saw a mother tigress covering her eighteen cubs. The cubs nuzzled close to her, but her milk was finished and they had nothing to drink. Exhausted, they were close to dying. The mother tigress was also on the brink of death; her flesh and blood had wasted away.

Seeing this, the princess felt unbearable compassion and thought, "I will offer them my own flesh and blood." Drawing closer, she made this aspiration:

> Triumphant buddhas of the past, present, and future—bear witness.
> When I offer my own body as a gift,
> may the tigress over there live and thrive!
> May my wish be fully accomplished.
> May I free all beings, as many as I can imagine,
> from the depths of the round of rebirth.

She lay down near them, but the tigress did not want to eat her. She and her cubs only smiled weakly. After that, the princess broke off a branch from a sandalwood tree. She used the wood to hack her own flesh into pieces, offering it to the tigers to nourish them back to health.

The princess's bones were visible and she was close to death. At that point, the tigress then recognized her as a carrier of the heritage of enlightenment. She collected water from sandalwood trees and nectar from flowers. Bathing the princess's gaping wounds, the tigress looked at the princess with such intense love that tears fell like rain from her eyes.

As soon as the princess regained her senses, she witnessed the tigress's extreme concern for her. "Even an animal like this is able to repay kindness done. She feels close to people who show love, and cares for humans who have helped her. How astonishing! If

I had died, I'm certain the tigress would have been crushed by grief at that moment and would have perished," she thought, feeling compassion.

Once her physical state improved, the princess raised herself onto her hands and feet. Clutching the branch of a sandalwood tree, she addressed the tigress:

> You roam among the jungle underbrush
> in forests of fragrant lotuses and sandalwood trees.
> At this moment, our fate has brought us together.
> Powerful mother tigress with your cubs,
> compelled by compassion and a wish to help you,
> I sliced my flesh to feed you
> with no thought for my own sake.
> I have no regrets: this saved your lives!
> Tigress mother and cubs,
> do not be concerned:
> I promise you I won't die.

The tigress understood the princess's words and smiled back at her.

After a few days passed, the princess's wounds were entirely healed. Her former good color and sweet scent returned, until she was just the same as before. The tigress wished to repay her kindness. Having seen the corpse of a fellow tigress who had died, she approached the princess and gestured repeatedly with her paws, until the princess followed and saw the corpse for herself.

The princess was overjoyed. "Now I can reach this spiritual attainment! I need to take the tigress's head and give it to the women adepts at the palace gate. Then I can enter and receive what I came for," she thought.

The princess cut the head from the corpse and bound it with bark from a sandalwood tree. Carrying it on her back, she approached the gate. Presenting the head to the gate-guardian adepts, she said, "I have what you asked of me. Here is the flesh of a tigress's head, so let me enter the palace."

A large adept replied, "I gladly accept this flesh. When you enter the palace, I will show you the way." She opened the gate, led the princess to a large, full square, and told her, "You stay here while I return to guard the gate."

The princess stood in the midst of a crowd of people and looked around. The group of people eyed her in turn. "A woman this attractive has never appeared here before. Why has she come?" they asked, bursting into raucous laughter.

The princess addressed everyone. "You have five distinctive and beautiful grand palaces surrounded by a vajra fence. You live in this impressive town amid a bounty of five kinds of flowers. A place like this inspires confidence and amazement. Can I meet your rulers? Who among you would be kind enough to lead me to them?"

One red woman said, "I will show you the way."

They went together to the palace veranda. There they saw some people being born amid joy, while others died weeping. Several people carried others as they flew into open space. Others were walking backward. Some enjoyed a feast of food and drink. A number had human bodies with animal heads. Others were arguing with one another or fighting in large armies.

Seeing all these things made the princess sad and uneasy. She asked her companion, "The way these people behave, the things they're doing here—it's all haphazard and doesn't fit together. What is this?"

The woman answered, "Your channels and circulating energies are disturbed and your mind is perceiving things impurely. Get ahold of yourself. Everyone gathered here is a hero or dakini by nature."

The princess asked, "When you say my channels and energies are disturbed, are you omniscient? Is this clairvoyance?"

The woman replied, "I know that your channels and energies are disturbed. I am clairvoyant, so listen to me as I explain.

"In the first eon, Buddha Boundless Light lived in a pure land called Lotus. This place was the source of all qualities without exception, a bountiful treasure trove akin to Unsurpassable Array

pure land. A magnificent prince named Radiant Gem lived there.
He had one thousand four daughters, the youngest of which was
called Sole Goddess Fire Light. Enthusiastic about spiritual practice, her main focus was compassion and generosity. She excelled
in perseverance and faith, which allowed her channel of sublime
insight to open.

"This woman venerated a teacher known as Imposing Lion. In
the first spring month, the eighth, fifteenth, and thirtieth days were
occasions to make abundant offerings and presentations of song
and dance, limitless in every direction.

"This woman wished to please her venerated teacher with the
most delicious and fragrant sap from a sandalwood tree. When
she went out to scrape sap from the tree, she found none on its
branches. Using a sharp blade, she cut the trunk at its roots. A
beautiful white goddess living there appeared. She held a nectar-
filled vase in her hands and asked, 'Why have you cut the trunk of
this sandalwood tree? Where have you come from?'

"The woman replied, 'I am the daughter of King Radiant Gem.
The teacher I venerate, Imposing Lion, is a buddha. This is an auspicious occasion to make abundant offerings to him. Only the most
delicious, exquisitely fragrant sap of a sandalwood tree will please
him. With that aim, I'm collecting some in order to honor and
serve my teacher for this celebration. I searched all the trees. Finding no sap on their leaves and branches, I cut this one.'

"Five-colored light radiated from the goddess's heart, suffus-
ing the upper limits of space. Everywhere the light reached filled
with emanations of the goddess and Buddha Limitless Light, who
intoned as one: 'Young woman, because you honor and serve your
teacher, any sincere aspiration you make will come to pass. For the
sake of all beings, make a sweeping aspiration without holding
back in any way.'

"The woman spoke, making this aspiration:

> I undertake this pure offering
> through the blessings of the truth

of the all-embracing expanse,
beyond center and bounds,
and through the immeasurable nondual compassion
of infinite buddhas.

I will make these pure offerings
and undertake inexhaustible positive acts
to cultivate the highest stores of goodness
for the sake of all beings, with none left out.
May I, together with every being,
reach unsurpassable, spontaneous bliss.

"The sincerity of the woman's aspiration led her to cultivate stores of goodness throughout innumerable lifetimes. That is how she was reborn as you, the princess, at this present time. She repeatedly possessed great wealth, which caused her to be reborn a princess to a present-day king.

"As a result of repeatedly serving and honoring her teacher in the past, you now make abundant offerings of service and faith in the present to Supreme Lotus-Born of Oddiyana. She repeatedly made previous aspirations; this now causes you to possess the nondual compassion of omniscience, by which you will serve beings in exceptional ways.

"Nevertheless, you were tainted by your mother's blood during your gestation in her womb, so you always witness the behavior of the six classes of beings. That cycle of delusion has disturbed the condition of your channels, energies, and vital essence. For that, meditate on vase breathing within your central channel. Do not focus your attention on your upper body; keep it directly on your navel. Settle within a state free of reference points."

The princess meditated on circulating energy according to the woman's instructions. This caused all the bizarre, vivid sights she had seen to fully resolve, down to the slightest. That gave rise to pure perception in her mind: she saw many groups of heroes and dakinis gathered on the palace veranda.

Then the woman said, "Princess, since you have directly resolved your channels, energies, and vital essence, you have been introduced to mother and child clear light. Therefore, we can both depart for the palace at the eastern gate."

They arrived at the eastern palace, where many dakinis were gathered. They were entirely white, like pure crystal. At the center of the palace rose a supreme sacred circle of the peaceful and wrathful deities. It was under a canopy of five-colored light, as if in a dreamscape.

Beside that sacred circle stood someone who said, "I am the awareness holder who dwells on enlightenment's stages." White in color, that awareness holder smiled radiantly and spoke to the princess and her companion. "I fully confer upon you both the twenty-one vase empowerments of the peaceful and wrathful deities, and assign you, Princess, the secret name Dorjé Düdul-ma, Vajra Demon Subduer."

Then the princess and her companion went to the palace at the southern gate. All the dakas and dakinis gathered inside were uniformly bright yellow. At the center of the palace rose a supreme sacred circle adorned with jewels. Beside the sacred circle stood someone who said, "I am the awareness holder with power over longevity." Yellow in color and showing the marks and signs of physical perfection, that awareness holder spoke to the princess and her companion. "I confer on you both the eleven empowerments for the vases of nectar held by Buddha Immortal."

Then they went to the western palace. It was flanked by a gathering of dakas and dakinis, all uniformly red, radiant, and smiling. A supreme sacred circle rose at the center of the palace, surrounded by a dense constellation of orbs, great and small. Beside that sacred circle stood someone who said, "I am the awareness holder of supreme seal." Red and beautifully radiant, the awareness holder spoke to the princess and her companion. "I confer upon you both the supreme illusion empowerment for the all-encompassing matrix of dakinis."

Then they went to the northern palace. All the dakas and dakinis gathered inside were green and presented themselves in a wrathful manner. At the center of that palace rose a supreme sacred circle covered with a mesh of weaponry. It was adorned with nets and half-nets of five-colored light; lotus flowers in five shades formed its perimeter. Beside that sacred circle stood someone who said, "I am the awareness holder of spontaneous ever-presence." Dark blue with a wrathful gaze, that awareness holder spoke to the princess and her companion. "I confer upon you both a major empowerment of awareness holders—the empowerment of the fourfold joy of great bliss."

Then they went to the central palace. All the dakas and dakinis gathered inside were the shade of ruby-colored lotus flowers. Alluringly lovely, their style shifted into anything at all, from peaceful to wrathful. At the center of the palace rose a supreme sacred circle. Entirely transparent from every vantage point, outside or in, it bore all the decorations typical of a charnel ground. The veranda was filled with crosshatched designs and dark canopies. Male and female awareness holders massed there like clouds, visibly feasting on nectar.

At the center of that sacred circle was someone who said, "I am the unsurpassable awareness holder, King Lord of the Dance." He shimmered with five-colored light and was entwined with his consort, a red dakini. She stood in a dancing pose, held a curved blade and skullcup, and had the posture of gazing into space. That awareness holder spoke to the princess and her companion, saying, "I confer upon you both the unsurpassable four empowerments of the awareness holders."

Afterward, her companion said, "Princess, listen to me. You persevered in the aspirations you made in the past and this is their true result in the present. You gained empowerment in the two aims, enlightenment for yourself and others. During this lifetime, you endured hardships for the sake of spiritual practice with no regard for your own life. You reached this land, Lotus Array, due to your stainless tantric bonds. If you do not recognize this place, listen as I explain.

"Nearly twelve months have passed in the human world since you arrived here from Chimpu charnel ground. This place is the site of the triumphant buddhas' blessings, so it's known as the western continent of bliss. Every male born here is a hero and every woman, a heroine. When they are hungry, they consume the food of tantric bonds at ritual feasts. When they are thirsty, they drink nectar. Their every act is the fearless conduct of those who dwell in meditative stability.

"That said, the one known as Abbot Lotus-Born of Oddiyana lives in the human land of Tibet. Since your share of spiritual attainment is there, you must return! This skullcup will provide you with many rations of food and drink. Keep hold of it and don't doubt yourself. Now bring to mind the forest charnel ground."

Her companion took a well-formed skullcup, wrapped it in a green cloth, and handed it to the princess, who said, "As a result of meeting an adept like you, I fully received every empowerment from each awareness holder in those palaces. What a great kindness! Would you allow me to live here, in this magnificent place? If I stay too long in Tibet, I'll encounter numerous problems."

The woman answered, "You cannot go against Lotus-Born of Oddiyana's command. Staying here would be a mistake. Go to Tibet and we will soon meet again. Later, you will rule this pure land of celestial enjoyment."

The princess held the skullcup. When she brought to mind the forest charnel ground of Chimpu, she arrived at her retreat cabin instantly.

After a year had passed, seven outlaw thieves appeared. The princess had three measures of flour to sustain her meditation practice. They stole it and demanded, "Young woman, what are you doing? What is your family line? What will you do with nothing to eat or drink? Your face is lovely and your manner reserved. You are easygoing, good at housework, and an expert cook. You are attractive to our eyes, yet you live in an empty, deserted land—that's sad! Follow us and you won't suffer from hunger and thirst."

At that moment, the princess meditated on Abbot Lotus-Born

of Oddiyana seated at the crown of her head. She wholeheartedly focused her body, speech, and mind with compassion on those hostile men. Meditating on the intention to awaken, she appealed to the nondual compassion of the triumphant buddhas for a way to avert this obstacle. Then she responded to the thieves.

"My family line is humble—that of meditative stability and meditation. The family line of my mother and father is despicable. If I have nothing to eat or drink, I will consume fruit juice. Given that I am a woman from a bad family, it's not right for us to associate with one another. You are at odds with my way of thinking; I don't care about those rations of flour that were my food. Since everything of substance is like wealth in a dream, I will explain how this is and all of you will listen!

> When you don't realize the domain of emptiness,
> this worldly realm is like a dreamscape.
> When you don't have the wealth of meditative stability,
> what you hoard in treasure vaults lasts as long as dew
>> on grass.
> If you do not integrate the appearances of wisdom with
>> your mind,
> the loved ones you cling to are like flowers carried off
>> by frost.
>
> When you miss the expanse of united emptiness and clarity,
> you possess the opposite of sublime insight,
> the seed of the round of rebirth.
>
> If you are not sheltered by a supremely kind lama,
> you are at the mercy
> of fiercely strong and potent negative forces
> who kill your compassion.

If you haven't gained stability
in meditative states without origin,
everything composite is like a mirage in space.

Since you outlaw thieves
do not enjoy spiritual practice,
you are like a pack of deranged beasts
roaming a barren valley.
People living without practicing
lead empty, wasted lives.

Your skill set is worthless.
I pity you outlaw thieves!
Do your eyes not see birth and death?
How do your minds tolerate pain and sickness?
Consider what you would want
and do not hurt others!

I gave up my life to endure hardship
for spiritual practice.
If you so desire,
you can eat my flesh and blood."

All the thieves felt regret and shame. Throwing their bodies on the ground, their tears flowed like blood. They wailed loudly with remorse for their previous wrongdoing, then took vows regarding their future actions. The thieves made aspirations, rejoicing in unsurpassable positive acts and casting away every activity of the round of rebirth.

Then, facing the nectar pill on her shrine, each offered a vow to endure hardship in spiritual practice for seven years. They stayed in retreat at the forest charnel ground of Chimpu, diligently meditating on the cycle of great perfection teachings for transformation from an ordinary state to a body free of defilements.

Seven months passed. On the morning of the tenth day of the lunar month, a large group of women appeared. They said, "Princess, together with the seven outlaw thieves, you meditated on your own bodies as masses of light and gained a degree of certainty. Come to the western land of Oddiyana for today's celebration."

The princess replied, "We have a vow to stay here in retreat. We can't go."

The women spread out a white silk cloth, insisting, "In any case, come sit on this seat."

Once the princess took her place, she told the seven outlaw thieves, "Come here and sit with me!" They left their retreat cabins and joined her.

Then the women lifted the edges of the white silk. They rose into open space and instantly arrived in the land of Oddiyana, in a place known as the meat-and-beer district. There, they saw a man called Awareness Holder with Topknot. He was resplendent and wore the trappings of a mantra adept. Groups of dakinis offered an immense ritual feast in his presence.

The awareness holder addressed the princess and the outlaw thieves. "Come here so we can talk," he said. When they approached him, at a distance of eight finger-widths from his heart, he revealed the sacred circle of spontaneously present peaceful and wrathful deities, the sacred circles of the awareness holders related to the eight deities of great accomplishment, and the sacred circle of the dakini cycle of Oceanic Great Bliss. He conferred upon them the complete empowerments for these practices. Then he assigned the princess the secret name Karchen Za, Lady of Karchen.

The seven thieves melted into light and dissolved into his heart. For the rest of the day, the princess and the awareness holder reveled in pleasure. After that, he had all the dakinis of that land gather for a day. He took the princess onto his lap while the dakinis all prostrated to them. "This is the Queen of Oddiyana," he said. Every last dakini offered prostrations and threw flowers toward her.

The awareness holder said to the princess, "All the triumphant buddhas of the past, present, and future consecrate you. You will definitely help beings. Take this well-formed skullcup and bring your home to mind." He gave her a white skullcup. Holding it in her hand, she thought of the charnel ground and arrived instantly back in Tibet in Chimpu. Only one day had passed since the princess went to the meat-and-beer district in Oddiyana.

After this, the princess stayed in retreat. Within ongoing clear light, she saw every realm of the six kinds of beings. Her intense compassion and disillusionment with the round of rebirth led her to make many sincere aspirations.

This concludes the second chapter, in which I, the princess, describe my voyages to the land of Oddiyana.

Samaya
Gya Gya Gya
Da-yik x5

3: The Princess Asks Lotus-Born of Oddiyana for Songs of Meditation Instruction

After a full twelve years had passed, Lotus-Born of Oddiyana returned from India to Tibet. The princess prostrated to him, imploring, "Supreme master, I respected your command and stayed in retreat for twelve years practicing great perfection. I also visited many places in the pure land of Oddiyana. The gateway of my experience and realization has begun to open. I am filled with great compassion for all beings of the three realms. I've also gained substantial certainty in the unsurpassable approach. Now do I completely comprehend every teaching of the supreme approach of secret mantra?"

"Listen to me, Princess," Lotus-Born of Oddiyana replied. "At this point, you have not reached a conclusion regarding the ground of our being according to secret mantra. When you fully comprehend the teachings of secret mantra, realization and omniscience arrive. As for what you've done so far, you have only a slight understanding of realization and omniscience. I will clarify this point. Listen to my song of experience:

> Consider what this means, Lady Lotus.
> When you reflect on death,
> that is the time to practice.
> Not only that,
> it's already almost too late.

I have words of heart advice for you,
so pay close attention
worthy and faithful woman,
and do as I say.

To begin, among the underlying causes
of the round of rebirth,
the mental afflictions of desire
cause utter misery.

In the cliff nests of the mountain of stupidity
dwell the small birds of ruinous anger.
They cling with bias to the roar of pride
and ride the gales of jealousy.

The mother who accompanies you is desire,
her children that you meet are mental clinging,
and the enemy you gain
is fixation on outer appearances.

When you ascribe singular existence
to what is nonexistent,
the round of rebirth's three realms arise
with its six kinds of beings.

Once you recognize this,
everything is an expression of oneness.
If you don't recognize this,
each and every suffering will be yours.

During the interim state,
you roam from place to place.
As soon as you encounter
the trigger of delusion,

both birth and decay come to pass,
leaving you burdened
with the karma of pain and sickness
in the ocean of death, transition, and misery.

This is how you are reborn into suffering.
Does your wild mind not see this?
Do not be numb to the teachings that inspire your faith.
You don't have time to be distracted, Lady Lotus.

If you lack stable footing
within the all-embracing expanse,
your mental consciousness is like a wind
blowing across the wide plain
of your repeated habitual actions.

These forceful circumstances—
your treacherous companions—
cleverly trick you as outer appearances.
Foster perseverance, Lady Lotus!

The vast round of rebirth
is deep and its shores are distant.
With its immense waves of misery
and mental affliction,
it's so easy for your childish mind to lose awareness.
This puts you at grave risk
of having it torn from your comfortable body.

Your laziness and lack of perseverance
will not lead to attaining enlightenment.
Whip your mind into shape, Lady Lotus.

Your practice, with the view and conduct separated,
treads the edge of a deep and narrow ravine.

Your parroting of teachings seems learned,
but you haven't invited the words into your mind.

Pay attention and cut dualistic mind at its root.
Now you have no choice
but to put this into practice.
Be relentless, Lady Lotus.

After he spoke, the princess fainted and collapsed; her body struck the ground. When she regained her composure, she said, "Supreme master, I beg you for a way to quickly free myself from the round of rebirth. How can I improve my meditation so I can escape this terrifying ravine? In all I've done, if I have completely missed the ultimate meaning of secret mantra, what is the right practice for me to do?"

Lotus-Born of Oddiyana addressed her:

Princess Lady Lotus,
your lineage and qualities are excellent,
so listen to me.

If you wish to escape the swamp
of the round of rebirth,
always stay in secluded mountain retreats
and keep in mind the acts of qualified lamas.

Faith is the fertile field of spiritual practice.
Make a resolution never to stray or waver from this.
Tantric bonds are the central pillar of spiritual attainment.
Come to a firm decision not to be hypocritical.

All beings have been your parents.
Foster compassion for them
and resolve not to be fickle in this.

Forbearance is your body's armor.
Decide to always make it meaningful.
Perseverance is the way to crush laziness.
Make a resolution not to procrastinate.

Courage is an unchanging bridge.
Firmly establish the meaning of meditative stability.
Clear light is the seed of the ground of our being.
Resolve to keep your sessions free of mental meddling.

Calm-abiding meditation is the road to rely on.
Decide to remain undistracted in post-meditative states.
Insight meditation is the ultimate summit.
Resolve not to harbor doubts or hesitation.

The phenomena of your six sensory avenues
are your own self-manifest expression.
Firmly resolve that this is the unborn nature of mind.
The five poisons are the five wisdoms,
which are the expression
of the five dimensions of enlightenment.
Come to the conclusion that they arise unimpeded,
free of attachment.

Consciousness determined by karma
is the expression of awareness.
Firmly resolve that the exhaustion of mind
is the all-embracing expanse.

The expanse and wisdom are indivisible,
the one thing released from all conditions.
That is empty clarity.
Come to the conclusion
that this is immediate awareness.

"Supreme Lotus-Born of Oddiyana, once I firmly establish awareness, in which appearances and mind are indivisible, what spiritual approach should I take?" the princess asked.

Lotus-Born of Oddiyana answered:

> Lady Lotus,
> worthy and faithful woman,
> listen to me.
>
> When disciples who are suitable recipients
> come to a conclusion regarding their fundamental nature
> and meditate on the unsurpassable approach
> of great perfection,
> it is not possible for them
> to miss the entryway to the path.
>
> However, for individuals who practice,
> the sacred doctrine of great perfection
> is not for those who keep the view and conduct
> separate and out of sync.
> People like that miss the entryway to the path.
>
> Great perfection is the best approach
> for those who live in accord with the teachings;
> it is not for groups of debaters and skeptics.
>
> As for people with karmic propensity
> who uphold their tantric bonds,
> and those who practice courageously in this life
> with faith and intact tantric bonds:
> these are the two groups
> meant to practice the supreme approach.
> They will establish great perfection's domain of meditation
> through its metaphors and meaning.

The symbols, meaning, and nature of reality
share the same essence.
Primordial purity is the empty expanse,
the surface of the sky.
Spontaneous ever-presence is empty and bright,
the lights of the sun and moon.
Their self-manifest expression
is unobstructed and moves everywhere.

Unite both cutting through resistance and direct vision;
have the appearances of the interim state
be perfected within the arena of direct vision;
then you empty the depths
of the round of rebirth and the worst hell.

That is the profound treasury of blissful Buddha Ever
    Excellent.
Whoever encounters these teachings
and upholds their tantric bonds is extremely fortunate.

"Supreme Lotus-Born of Oddiyana, the doctrine of great perfection is a profound, unsurpassable treasury," the princess said,
asking, "When I cultivate my experience of this supreme approach,
in what places should I live? Will these practice places, charnel
grounds, clay sites, mountain ranges, slate cliffs, forest hermitages,
and mountain flanks increase my experience? What is the tech-
nique to have realization born in my mind?"
Lotus-Born of Oddiyana responded:

Lady Lotus, you are a qualified woman
with noble intent, so listen to me.

When fortunate people put into practice
the supreme approach of great perfection,

snow mountain ranges are pure places;
their slate cliffs are also suitable for meditation.

In brief, stay in places where dissolutionment is born.
The clay and slate
of deserted snow mountain ranges
are naturally blue in color.
When the sky is clear and clean,
mist and clouds vanish in space.

When you sit at sunrise and sunset
during the season of golden autumn,
which is neither summer nor winter,
meditate with the eyes of the nature of reality.

In a secluded place,
witness your fundamental nature
and come to the conclusion
that it is the empty expanse of primordial purity.

The inner radiance of emptiness
is outwardly complete as the five lights,
the expression of awareness.

When the stirring of your karmic energies
is exhausted in the expanse of space,
you will see clear light
within the five interim states.

Cut the chains of calm-abiding meditation.
Destroy the spear of the mountain
of insight meditation.
Crush the foe—investigation.

Be decisive regarding the manifest nature of reality.
Mind and appearances are stainless,
free of dross.
This is empty clarity—
how very fortunate you are!

The princess asked, "Supreme Lotus-Born of Oddiyana, while cultivating my experience of the doctrine of great perfection, what kind of lama should I rely upon to expose awareness?"
Lotus-Born of Oddiyana responded:

Lady Lotus, you are a princess of an excellent line
and a qualified woman,
so listen to me.

When meditating on the supreme approach
of great perfection,
it is especially valuable to rely constantly on lamas
for enriching your experience
and dispelling obstacles.

These are the qualifications of such lamas:
Their lineage endows them
with blessings and great compassion.
They have met the deity face-to-face
and gained spiritual attainment.
They are replete with the blessings
and prophecies of the dakinis.

These lamas are skilled in the meaning of empowerments
that lead to spiritual maturity
and expert at giving practical instructions
that lead to liberation.
They possess the complete qualities
of learning, contemplation, and knowledge.

Because they have realization,
they are free from doubts.
They skillfully nurture disciples
in harmony with the doctrine
of united emptiness and compassion.
High-minded in their approach,
they scarcely entertain attachment.

Whoever has those characteristics
is an effective lama.
When you stay close to them,
spontaneous experiences will effortlessly arise
and the vajra strand of awareness
will grow in the arena of direct vision,
the all-embracing expanse of liberation.
Such lamas hold the meaning
of the view of great perfection.

Again, the princess asked, "Supreme Lotus-Born of Oddiyana,
when cultivating my experience of the teachings of great perfection, what characteristics should my spiritual companions have?"
Lotus-Born of Oddiyana answered:

Lady Lotus, you are a qualified woman
with faith, so listen to me.

Your spiritual companions
should have these favorable characteristics:
faith, forbearance of suffering,
great compassion,
as well as pure tantric bonds and few preoccupations.

Their respectful devotion is stable,
so they are able to keep secrets
and have minimal attachment
to appearances and consciousness.

Impeccable in regard to karma,
they keep a humble position
and are steadfast in practice.

They reflect on good and bad acts,
and are open-minded, easygoing, and even-tempered.
They gracefully navigate everyday life's connections,
know the difference between spiritual approaches,
and easily engage with all experience and realization.

Your companions aspire to serve beings,
don't subscribe to debate jargon,
and keep their plans and busyness to a minimum.
Never scornful or doubtful,
they show scant bias toward those who offer approval.

Such companions are intent
on fostering the sole heritage of enlightenment.
Major distractions bother them;
they stay in secluded places
and feel little anger and pride.

When you depend on such excellent companions,
they are the field in which every quality grows.
Stay close to them always,
no matter what,
and sustain yourself on true happiness and good qualities.
They will be a second lama
for your meditative concentration.

Once again, the princess asked, "Supreme Lotus-Born of Oddiyana, when cultivating my experience of the doctrine of great perfection, what is the sacred practice of activity for everyday life?"
Lotus-Born of Oddiyana replied:

Lady Lotus, woman of an excellent line,
you have faith, so listen to me.

For great perfection meditation,
I will explain the best activity for everyday life
and you should do as I say.

The sacred circles within your own body
hold luminous orbs,
pure lands where dakas and dakinis
reside in union,
fully present of their own accord.

Your brain's immeasurable skull mansion
holds fifty-eight fierce blood-drinkers.
Bow to Supreme Blood-Drinker,
male and female in union,
and delight them with a ritual feast of nectar.
The immeasurable mansion at your heart
hosts forty-two peaceful buddhas.
Delight them with offerings
of your meditation.

An orb in each of your six channel wheels
is one of six adepts who manifests to guide beings.
Delight them with nourishing food.

Use the three gazes
to look into clear, stainless space
applying this all-inclusive single point:
meditate on the five colors
of empty clarity's indwelling glow,
the orbs and deity forms,
and your vajra strand of awareness.

Come to the firm conclusion
that this is the manifest nature of reality.

Do this sacred practice four sessions a day
and enjoy four ritual feasts.
Cultivate the meditative state
and hear naturally resounding mantra
within the indivisible union
of the deity and the nature of reality.

Carrying out these four kinds of activity,
decide that mind and appearances, indivisible,
are the essence of the ground of our being.

When you reach the consummation of the four visions,
this will carry you to the expanse,
where everything is exhausted.
Settle within your unfabricated fundamental nature
while you watch awareness's unimpeded avenue of arising.

Merge past, present, and future thoughts
with the united expanse and awareness,
relaxing at ease in this unfabricated state.

This singular pith of the nature of mind
is not a momentary flash;
it has always been available.
Never contrived,
it arises of itself.
While it is empty,
the inner glow of its emptiness
is, by nature, clarity—
vivid, fresh, and unveiled.

Appearances of the ground of our being
and the path—
these share a single essence
that is not burdened by circumstances
or moved by causes.

Always keep hold of this meaning
as the lasting foundation of awareness.
The union of conduct and the view
is the path of great perfection.

"Supreme Lotus-Born of Oddiyana, when cultivating my experience of the teachings of great perfection, how can I enrich my practice?" the princess asked.

Lotus-Born of Oddiyana responded:

You are a princess who carries
the heritage of enlightenment,
so listen to me.

When those who carry
the heritage of enlightenment
meditate on great perfection,
their meditation should include
the sacred practice of the channels,
vital essence, and circulating energies.
This is an exceptional way
to travel to enlightenment.

Cultivate this profound domain of experience:
with a goddess manifested from your heart,
revel in enjoyment with her
and then reverse and spread the vital essence.
This will carry you to the expanse
of the exhaustion of your circulating energies,

the ultimate, formless dimension.
The inseparable three dimensions
of enlightenment are great bliss.

Rely on uncontaminated wisdom
to merge bliss with the expanse
of the realm of emptiness and primordial purity.
Immerse yourself in the vault of the essence, bliss.
Furthermore, when you practice
with a young, attractive companion,
their age should be between sixteen
and twenty-five, not more.

In the midst of bliss,
their skin flushes
as they make amorous sounds
and move in pleasure.
They ought to have a pale, rosy complexion.

Steeped in faith, sublime insight,
and substantial compassion,
they will be broad-minded,
able to keep secrets,
and not prone to chatter.
They should have a dignified manner
and not be possessive of you.

When you rely on someone with those traits
as your companion for this practice,
the fivefold exercises of the channels
will close the gateway of grasping to defilements.
Once you send both of your vital essences
and draw them back up,
envelop the pangs of desire with bliss.

These three methods
of drawing and binding your circulating energy
arrest the movement of impure mind,
ignite the bliss and heat
of the five wisdoms and dimensions of enlightenment,
and condense the pith meaning of all teachings.

Firmly resolve that the essence of great bliss
overwhelms ordinary practice with splendor,
forcefully perfects all deity and mantra practice,
allows you to move unimpeded through the five elements,
and makes you expert in displays
of predictive sight and clairvoyance.

The vault of clear light
holds both appearances and awareness
as you reach the full measure
of the sole and supreme culmination of the path.

Take these exercises for your channels,
vital essence, and circulating energies
and integrate them with your practice of the four lamps.
That is the highest summit
of ways to enrich your practice.

Furthermore, the princess asked, "Supreme Lotus-Born of Oddiyana, what are the indications and measures of reaching the completion of great perfection?"

Lotus-Born of Oddiyana answered:

Princess, lovely woman of an excellent line
who makes sounds in the midst of pleasure,
listen to me.

As fortunate disciples
cultivate their experience
of the superlative doctrine of great perfection,
when day and night
merge with clear light and bliss,
this indicates gaining stability within the essence.

Reaching the full measure
of unchanging empty awareness
indicates that you've entered into the expanse
of the indwelling nature of all things.

Understanding worlds and their residents
as a dance of magical illusion
indicates that you've reached
the full measure of nondual compassion.

When you gain mastery of the four lamps,
come to the conclusion that these pure lands
are fully present of their own accord.

When you indivisibly unite appearances and mind,
you will gracefully navigate everyday life's
causes, conditions, and connections.

When you complete the vision
of the manifest nature of reality,
you have arrived at the point of increasing experience.
When you reach the full measure of awareness,
you attain the truth of the exhaustion
of the nature of reality.

When you gain mastery
of these four visions to their fullest degree,

your intrinsic deity nature
will be stable during the interim state;
you will discover the pure lands,
dimensions of enlightenment, and rays of light.

This dust-free sky that appears outside you
means that your life-force circulating energy
is exhausted in the vase of your central channel.
This fivefold movement
of your body's karmic circulating energy
is naturally pure
and freed in the expanse of your heart.

You will discover the light
of your flesh, blood, and breath,
and that of the five elements
that make up the world.

Seeing the seed at your channel wheels
gains you the potency
of mother and child clear light;
as you transform from an ordinary state
to a body free of defilements,
it will dissolve into a body of light.

With unimpeded omniscience
in regard to past, present, and future,
your emanations demonstrate infinite ways of appearing,
differentiating between the graded approaches
of all spiritual teachings.
You gain mastery over the unobstructed space
of experience and conduct.

Never departing from the empty clarity
of the nature of reality,

the five deity forms will appear distinctly
from something as minute as the tiniest grain.
With that exhaustion of dualistic appearances,
great bliss will arise and you will experience bliss.
Know the meaning of these measures
and indications of your practice.

The princess asked, "Supreme Lotus-Born of Oddiyana, for
those disciples who never waver in cultivating their experience of
the doctrine of great perfection, how do we get free of dying and
the interim state?"
Lotus-Born of Oddiyana answered:

You are a princess who carries
the heritage of enlightenment.
Whether or not you understand my explanations,
listen now.

Everyone who fails to gain mastery
of the united expanse and awareness
is subject to birth, death, and transition.
Those who practice great perfection
are extremely fortunate.

When your breathing stops at the end of life,
your outward breath draws together and dissolves.
All your faculties dim
as your inner air is lost far away.
In your subjective experience,
you see only the manifestation of your karma.

Once your mind's life force
is stunned into blankness,
vivid awareness is the clear-light child
who is the bright arising

of awareness's outward radiance.
Together with that is peace,
the empty-expanse mother,
who is limpid awareness without fixation,
an expression of the ultimate.

The most powerful conduct is clear omniscience.
Wakeful resting within this is natural meditation.
Dwelling there without movement
is the confidence of the view.

The dance of the ultimate,
formless dimension of enlightenment
transcends everything.
The basic character of the form dimension of complete
    enjoyment
is bliss, the realm of emptiness.
The form dimension of manifest embodiment
appears to anyone as anything at all.

Nothing can be expressed within that profound meaning.
This is the superlative doctrine of great perfection,
the supreme, secret, sovereign approach.

It is not an experience accessible to lesser individuals.
The reward for fortunate ones,
it is unlike anything ordinary.
For those who see, touch, recall, or think of this,
it brings great bliss.

For those at the lowest level,
this will purify their experience of the interim state.
Those of middle level will be shown
the nature of reality in the interim state.

Those of the highest level will not experience the interim
    state,
as sight and liberation will be simultaneous.

"Supreme Lotus-Born of Oddiyana, the doctrine of great perfection is the summit of all practices, but does not knowing how
to meditate lead to obstacles or not?" the princess asked. "Are there
degrees of acumen or not? Are mind and appearances defined by
a single characteristic or not? Is gaining spiritual attainment contingent on time or not?"

Lotus-Born of Oddiyana responded:

Princess, you are a worthy recipient
of these tantric teachings.
Listen undistracted as I, Lotus,
explain these points.

When great perfection,
the highest teachings,
is related to individuals,
it is necessary to apply a framework for practice.

This is the way of great perfection:
hold your body unmoving as you maintain the gazes;
keep your voice silent without uttering a thing;
keep your mind at rest with no plans.

Do not control your breathing;
let it be natural.
Once you expose the united expanse and awareness,
meditate on that.
Anyone in tune with making this their experience
will not be crushed by obstacles.
Merely seeing great perfection itself
is said to be meaningful.

As for individuals having different degrees of acumen,
everyone is fine.
Moreover, anyone can be assured of liberation
when they transform from an ordinary state
to a body free of defilements.

Mind and appearances
are not two separate things.
For the nature of mind,
clinging is a temporary condition
whose expression creates the impression
of things outside yourself.
If temporary dualistic mind is purified,
then appearances are purified.

What we call wisdom
is the inner glow of emptiness.
Whoever reveals that is a buddha.
Moreover, they adjust their teachings
to each context to expertly guide beings:
this is superb nondual compassion.

As for whether gaining spiritual attainment
is contingent on time,
for anyone fortunate enough
to take as their experience
the indivisible expanse and awareness,
it is not.

Whoever has devotion and intact tantric bonds
already holds the vase that grants spiritual attainment.
Whoever continuously meditates on great perfection
becomes a lord of twofold spiritual attainment.

To summarize, I gave you the inner pith of great perfection,
the heart of all teachings.
If I were to expand on this teaching,
it would make it more complex.
When synthesized,
it is easy to put into practice.

It is minimally challenging,
greatly meaningful,
and easy to understand.
Don't let your mind fall under the sway
of other things you see and hear.

Princess, when you
put these teachings into practice,
have faith, be diligent,
and do not become numb
as you meditate on undefiled great bliss.

Immediately, the princess's analytical outlook ceased and she was relieved of her blind meditation. Gaining certainty in great perfection, she achieved the transformation from an ordinary state to a body free of defilements, and gained the spiritual attainment of life free of birth and death.

This concludes the third chapter, in which I, the princess, ask Lotus-Born of Oddiyana for songs of meditation instruction.

Samaya
Gya Gya Gya

4: The Princess Receives the Scriptures and Transmissions for the Nine Levels of Approach from Lotus-Born of Oddiyana

From Supreme Lotus-Born of Oddiyana, the princess received the entire doctrine of great perfection, with nothing left out, at Gegong Cave in Samyé Chimpu charnel ground.

At Slate Cliff, she received an entire cycle of *The Collection of Supreme Bliss* centered on the hundred peaceful and wrathful deities.

At Symbol of Dakini Script charnel ground, she received an entire cycle of *Ocean of Dakinis*.

At Secret Wisdom Cliff Cave, she received the entire cycle of *Awakened Hero Supreme Nondual Compassion, Lord Protector of Loving-kindness*.

At Officials' Neck Clay Hermitage, she received general predictions for the doctrine and specific predictions for certain individuals. She also received in their entirety the important discourses for some specific levels of Buddhist systems.

In Samyé, at Purification Temple and Central Temple, she received *Highest Scripture on the Monastic Code of Conduct, Advice for Novices—Radiant Discipline, Holy Scripture on the Monastic Code of Conduct, An Extensive Commentary to "The Root Discourse on Monastic Discipline,"* and other teachings that constitute the doctrine of the listener attendants.

At Manjushri Temple in Samyé, she received instruction in the pure twelve links of interdependent causation and other teachings that constitute the entire doctrine of the self-reliant buddhas.

At Maitreya Temple in Samyé, she received *The Flower Ornament Discourse*, *The Great Transcendence of Sorrow Discourse*, *The Mound of Jewels Collection of Discourses*, *The Journey to Langka Discourse*, *The Perfection of Sublime Insight in 100,000 Stanzas*, and other teachings that constitute the entire doctrine of awakened heroes.

At Meditative Concentration Temple in Samyé, she received *The Susiddhi-kara Tantra*, *The Sublime Awareness Supreme Tantra*, *The Tantra Requested by Subahu*, *The Vajra Holder Empowerment Supreme Tantra*, and other teachings that constitute the entire doctrine of Kriyayoga, the sacred practice of outward action.

In the grand middle level of Jokhang Central Temple, she received *The Tantra of the Very Extensive Sovereign Lord Discourse Emanated and Blessed by Supreme Illuminator's Manifest, Perfect Awakening*; *Brilliant Sun Tantra*; *Victory Over the Three Worlds Tantra*; and other teachings that constitute the entire doctrine of Upayoga, the sacred practice of conduct.

There, she also received *The Precious Gathering of Transcendent Buddhas Tantra*; *Sangraha Tantra*; *Brilliantly Radiant Transcendent Buddhas Tantra*; *Transcendent Honored One, Genuine Perfectly Enlightened One Who Completely Cleanses All Miserable Existences, Segment of the Lustrous King Tantra*; *Illustrious Sublime First One, Sovereign Segment of the Great Way Tantra*; *Victorious Wrathful Deity Tantra*; and other teachings that constitute the entire doctrine of Yoga Tantra, the continuum of sacred practice.

Before the Jowo Statue in Central Temple, she received the wisdom-body text of union, *Illustrious Equal Union of All Buddhas, Dakini Sublime Bliss of Illusion Latter Tantra*; the wisdom-speech text of liberation, *Secret Moon Vital Essence, Wisdom Speech Tantra*; the wisdom-mind text of the unique sphere, *Matrix of Mystery—Supreme Sovereign Segment*; *Net of Illusion, Supreme Sovereign Tantra*; *The Highest Net of Illusion Tantra*; the text on astrological sciences, *Illustrious Vajra Four Seats—Sovereign of Yogini Tantras*; *Tantra Blazing Like the Fires at the End of Time*;

Custom of Spiritual Practice of the Vajra Family, Wrathful Pundarika Tantra; Nonstraying Jewel Tantra; Display of the Secret Sublime Horse; Nonstraying Goddess Tantra; Gathering of Illustrious Blood-Drinkers—Root Tantra; Tantra of the Slayer of the Lord of Death; Tantra of the Transmission of Mundane Existence; The Eight Volumes; and other teachings that constitute the entire doctrine of Mahayoga, the great sacred practice.

At Hepori Mountain Peak, she received *Secret Essence, Definite Suchness Sovereign Tantra; Illusion Tantra; Illusion Tantra—the Remaining Chapters; Lotus Garland, Exalted Lasso of Skillful Means Tantra;* and other teachings that constitute the entire doctrine of Anuyoga, the following sacred practice.

At Awakened Medicine Peak, she received the text on the view, *Vajrasattva Supreme Space, Secret Essence, Meaning of the Natural State Tantra;* the text on meditation, *Meditation on Awakened Mind Tantra; Auspicious Glory, Cuckoo of Awareness Tantra; Revealing the Meaning of Supreme Bliss Tantra; Entering All Domains Tantra;* and other teachings that constitute the entire doctrine of Atiyoga, the pinnacle sacred practice.

At sites all around Samyé, she received in their entirety the lesser teachings of the nine approaches simply through devotion.

At Chimpu Ke-u Gong, she received the innermost secret unsurpassable teachings [the seventeen great perfection tantras of the pith instructions], which encompass the entire cycle of instructions on every meaning of the great approach.

Particularly at Rocky Chimpu charnel ground, she received the lama's own doctrinal cycle—Great Gem Treasure Vault; the cycle of Wisdom Light Treasury related to the chosen deities; and the cycle of Secret Great Bliss related to the dakinis. Moreover, she also received many cycles related to the accomplished awareness holders.

At every major and minor sacred site, including Tildro White Cliff, Tsari Yagong Site, Sha-ug Tak Go, Koting Enclosure, Taktsang Sengé Dzong, Yangleshö, Gawa Tsal, Silwa Tsal, Bheta Rocky Cave, and Thousand Lotus Cave, she received all the meditation advice and teachings for each spiritual approach, as well as the pith instructions, until she was sated.

"Any place filled by the emanations of Lotus-Born of Oddiyana, I, the princess, was also there, filling it with my emanations as his followers who requested teachings. Whatever Supreme Lotus-Born of Oddiyana taught, I fully comprehended. I acquired all the major general teachings of the great approach, as well as those of great perfection, the wisdom of the union of the expanse and awareness. I was introduced to mind and wisdom as the ultimate, formless dimension of enlightenment.

"The omniscient lord of the past, present, and future, Lotus-Born himself, Abbot of Oddiyana, granted me the entire, complete teachings of the nine levels of spiritual approach. This led me to a firm conclusion regarding my own secret fundamental nature, and I was introduced to mother and child clear light."

This concludes the fourth chapter, in which I, the princess, receive the scriptures and transmissions for the nine levels of spiritual approach from Lotus-Born of Oddiyana.

Samaya
Gya Gya Gya

5: THE PRINCESS HELPS OTHERS
IN THE HELL REALM

One night at Chimpu, in the secret cave of Ke-u Gong, a group of women gathered to offer the ritual feast. Our ranks included a great number of qualified adepts: me, the princess; Pema Sal, the daughter of the king of Samyé; Princess Trompa Gyan; Nujin Salé; Lekjin Zangmo; Lady Dorjé Tso; Shelkar Za, the main consort of Lotus-Born of Oddiyana; the Chaplain of Chokro; Lady Ting Yangma of Drom; Rinchen Tsün of Chokro; Rinchen Salé Ö; and Lady Matima of Ru-yong. We arranged seven golden turquoise mandalas, offered them to Lotus-Born of Oddiyana, and addressed him in unison: "Supreme Lotus-Born of Oddiyana, we women have taken a low birth, yet we hold ourselves in high regard. Our character is spoiled and our knowledge is trivial, so we need teachings that aren't difficult but have great meaning. We implore you: grant us your sacred advice for attaining swift enlightenment, care for us kindly, and nurture us with your nondual compassion."

Lotus-Born of Oddiyana replied, "Faithful women with noble intent, listen to me. To attain swift enlightenment, you must enter the doorway of the adamantine approach of secret mantra. Once you have, never break your tantric bonds, and be stable within the ultimate, indivisible expanse and awareness. When you transform from an ordinary state to a body free of defilements, you will become enlightened within the union of emptiness and clarity, the expanse of the five lights."

Then he revealed twenty-five sacred circles for *Great Array of Chittiyoga, Luminous Expanse of Great Perfection*. He gave these empowerments as practice instructions. Based on that, this group cultivated their experience in meditation for one month. During that time, each woman saw one of the five aspects [body, speech, mind, qualities, and activities] of the five pure lands, fully present of their own accord, each representing one of the same five aspects: these women became the twenty-five accomplished female adepts.

Many others became the eighty-one accomplished male adepts, including Bendé Sangyé Yeshé, Namkhai Nyingpo, Ngen-lam Gyalwa Chok-yang, Atsara Salé, Berotsana, Kawa Paltsek, Chokro Lui Gyaltsen, Prince Mutik Tsenpo, Chokdrub Tsal, and Tre-u Chung.

Specifically in regard to the princess, after she had been practicing for a week, a wrathful creature appeared at night in front of her retreat cabin. His dark-blue body was the same size as the sky and he held a curved blade and skullcup filled with blood. "Princess, you've mastered everything you needed to attain enlightenment, but are you able help others?" he asked.

She answered, "I can help! Please tell me the pure land where I will find my disciples."

The wrathful man replied, "Princess, if you're able to serve others, in that case, you should go to hell. Earlier in your life, someone blocked your path to awakening. That evil official, whose name is Shanti, is below us right now. Due to the weight of his evil, he's suffering down there in the Hell of Endless Torment, so you need to lead him out of this misery and protect him. Take this road to hell."

With that, a gaping, black void opened up, with a white ladder leading downward. When the wrathful man pointed to it, the princess entered the opening and climbed down the ladder. She saw a black iron mountain. It was flanked by an army of many thousands of devils surrounding crowds of people. The devils drilled holes in their heads, hammered scores of iron spikes into their feet, and further tortured them by smashing their heads with hammers. The devils shouted, "This is for what you've done. From now on, we're going to torture you!" and those people wailed loudly.

The princess asked that devil army, "What did these people do? Is an evil official named Shanti here?"

Among them, one short, hunchbacked devil with red eyes told her, "While these people were humans, they killed living creatures, from the smallest to the largest ones, including goats, sheep, and pigs. This is the result. Shanti isn't here. The place below here is called 'the Hell of Crying Out.' He likely went there."

The princess descended and saw an immense copper cauldron the size of a plain sitting atop three giant red mountains. The cauldron was filled to the brim with water. The blazing fire underneath made the water roil, churn, and boil. In the cauldron, the blistering hot, bubbling water cooked masses of people. They wailed loudly and shrieked, "What have we done to deserve this?"

An army of many thousands of devils carrying iron hammers surrounded them. They pounded the heads of the people in the cauldron, shouting, "You've brought this on yourselves so you should be satisfied. From now on, we're going to hit you."

The princess asked that devil army, "What did these people do? Is an evil official named Shanti here?"

Among them, one of their leaders had an ox's head and a wooden cane propped up beneath his chin. He told her, "While these people were humans, they took for themselves the wealth of the spiritual community, and beat and harmed many living beings. They also made the buddhas bleed with malicious intent. This is the result of their actions, but Shanti isn't here. The place below here is called 'the Hell of Extreme Red Fire.' He's likely there."

The princess descended and saw a hot plain of red iron filings, upon which many people were roasting and convulsing. Their bodies were split into pieces vertically and horizontally, their limbs burned into ash, and their bones became black charcoal. They shrieked, "Owww! We're in so much pain," and wailed loudly. Around them an army of one thousand devils shouted, "You've brought this on yourselves!" as they flayed their skin with sharp razor blades.

The princess asked those devils, "What did these people do? Is an evil official named Shanti here?"

Among them was one devil with an excellent black body and

a bear's head, holding a trident. He told her, "When these people lived in the human realm, they cultivated corrupt views and allowed their tantric bonds related to the wisdom body to decline. This is the result of their actions, but Shanti isn't here. Below here is a place called 'the Hell of Endless Torment.' He's there, so go down to that place."

The princess descended and saw the ground there entirely aflame. At its center stood a blazing-hot iron building without any doors. Coming from inside, she heard loud wails and cries of "We're in so much pain!"

An army of many hundreds of thousands of devils engulfed the building. The devils impaled the people's stomachs with tridents, hammered spikes through their heads and beat them, marked their bodies with lines and tore them asunder, gouged their eyes out with a long needle, and drank their blood. Under them they lit fires, and above them, they poured molten red iron. Using swords and spears, the devils dismembered and scattered the people's limbs in every direction.

A hole one arm-span wide gaped open on the iron building's side. The devils around it dragged each person inside out through that opening, one at a time. They hacked the people to pieces, feasted on their flesh, and guzzled their blood. Flaying the skin from the soles of their feet, the devils used red meteorite metal to iron their legs until the cartilage was exposed, then they sucked it out. They pinned them down with hundreds of iron spikes in each of their limbs and beat them.

Crying, "This is our fate!" they wailed loudly. The devil army impaled them, front to back and back to front, with tridents and nine-pronged spears, shouting, "You've brought this on yourselves, so you should be satisfied! From now on, we're going to beat you."

The princess asked these devils, "What did these people do? Is an evil official named Shanti here?"

Among that army was one devil with a lion's head who was holding a sharp spear. He told her, "When these people were humans, they had a corrupt view toward the Three Jewels and the adepts who had gained realization of their fundamental nature. They created obstacles to others' positive acts. This is the result. As for this evil official named Shanti, I will go see if he's here or not."

He entered the iron building. When he emerged, he said, "Shanti is here. What business do you have with him?"

The princess answered, "When this evil official was a human, he was incredibly cruel. He also caused obstacles to my path to awakening. He's trapped here as a result of those actions. I have such intense compassion within me that it's unbearable. Therefore, I've come to take on the burden of his share of suffering and lead him to a state of lasting happiness. Let Shanti out and I will take his place. Help me!"

The devil replied, "I can't do that. You have to ask the king in person." He led the princess and they approached someone the devil called "the King of Karma." That black king had a massive body, an ox's head, and a piercing gaze. He held a wide, flat board with crosshatched markings.

The king asked, "What are you doing here, Princess? There is nothing but suffering in this horrific place, and it's all caused by individuals' repetitive negative acts."

The princess replied, "Great King, listen to me. This vicious official named Shanti did only evil for as long as he lived. When I learned that he had gone from the human realm to the hells, I came to take on his share of suffering and lead him to a state of lasting happiness. I beg of you: Is there any way to send him back to the human realm?"

The king answered, "What you're saying is all very well. However, he accumulated his own bad karma, so as much as you try to help him, it will only cause him harm. I have no ill will toward him, but it's his bad karma to bear. If you take on his suffering, it will harm this evildoer even more. That said, if you know the ritual of the peaceful and wrathful deities to empty the depths of hell, it is powerful and beneficial."

The princess then nourished her meditative state and entered into meditation. In front of the iron building, she set up the sacred circle of one hundred one peaceful and wrathful deities. When she prostrated to it, the iron building split into a hundred pieces. All the fire's sharp heat and every weapon vanished without a trace. The temperature entirely evened out, and everyone felt physically, verbally, and mentally happy.

The army of devil minions also smiled peacefully and became helpful. One million, one hundred thousand hell-beings, including the evil official Shanti, were protected by the infinite victorious peaceful and wrathful deities, then placed in a pure land.

Even the king, the master of hell, prostrated to the princess and said, "You are kind to everyone. Your incredible nondual compassion is greater than that of all previous buddhas. When you return to the human realm, show others the sacred circle of the infinite peaceful and wrathful deities."

The princess made aspirations and uplifted her mind to awakening. Then she ascended to Chimpu, arriving in front of her retreat cabin in the charnel ground, as before. Standing in front of the door, she saw the same wrathful creature who spoke to her earlier. He asked, "Princess, did you get that evil official Shanti out of the hell realm?"

She answered, "I placed many hell-beings, including him, into a state of lasting happiness, as you requested."

He said, "You've gained mastery of realization. In the space of the nature of reality, you move with the force of the wisdom of awareness. Your nondual compassion nourishes beings and is victorious over all suffering. Therefore, your nondual compassion is stronger than that of all peaceful and wrathful triumphant buddhas, including Lord Heruka. I am giving you the name Dakini Yeshé Tsogyal, Victorious Ocean of Wisdom." After he spoke, that wrathful creature dissolved without a trace into Tsogyal's heart.

Supreme Lotus-Born of Oddiyana also praised Tsogyal:

> You are a fully qualified dakini
> and the mother who gives life
> to all triumphant buddhas.

Yours is the great force of all buddhas,
as the motherly loving protector
of all beings of the six realms.

My own qualities as Lotus-Born
don't come from me—
they come from you.
You are the source of all qualities
and the treasury of spiritual attainments that grant bliss.
You have gained the state
of a spontaneous awareness holder
with power over longevity.
In this very lifetime,
you've perfected the great perfection teaching
for attaining the undefiled body.

Until the depths of cyclic existence are emptied,
you will continuously emanate in every land.
Your nondual compassion
will transform into anything at all.
Your supreme enlightened line
is that of Buddha Lady Ever-Excellent.
You are spontaneous great bliss.
I hail you as the peerless dakini.

This concludes the fifth chapter, in which I, the princess, help others in the hell realm.

Samaya
Gya Gya Gya
Da-yik x5

6: The Princess Receives Prophecies

Lotus-Born of Oddiyana went on to give the princess these prophecies:

"Dakini Yeshé Tsoygal, during this lifetime, in your self-perception, you will be equal to Buddha Lady Ever-Excellent. Concerning what appears to others when that happens, you will send as many emanations as possible to guide beings in any way necessary; your emanations will be inconceivable. Each one will appear before each being throughout hundreds of millions of worlds. As you show yourself in whatever way is necessary to guide others, you will place anyone connected to you in the state of the exhaustion of the nature of reality.

"In sum, until you empty the depths of cyclic existence, you will serve beings in deeply meaningful ways and will bring them to spiritual maturity through empowerments and to liberation through guidance in tantric practice.

"Furthermore, all phenomena of the round of rebirth and transcendent states originate from our own minds. Therefore, it is crucial to know our minds' faults.

"As you apply the key points of the profound pointing-out instructions, you must be relentless in your practice. If you don't carry it to its conclusion, the poisonous corpse of your thoughts will linger. This is like having the remains of a disease lodged within you.

"When you take temporary, ethereal meditative experiences as the best possible state, and adopt an attitude filled with positive thoughts, the outcome of such practice will be nothing more than rebirth in the higher realms. It is crucial to know the faults of holding on to meditative experience.

"Princess, since you've realized the meaning of the two truths, ceaselessly reincarnate until you empty the depths of cyclic existence. In particular, the lowest point in the duration of the Buddha's doctrine will come during the spread of the fivefold degeneration. At that time, an incarnation of your wisdom body will be invested by the signs of the five buddha families. Any degree of connection to this individual will be meaningful. This person's area of activity will be the Himalayan region, in central Tibet.

"An incarnation of your wisdom speech will be invested by the lamas and dakinis. This worthy individual's area of activity will be in western Tibet, in Tsang.

"An incarnation of your wisdom mind will be invested by the Three Jewels. Any degree of connection with this individual will lead beings to the celestial pure land. This incarnation's area of activity will be eastern Tibet, in Kongpo.

"An incarnation of your wisdom qualities will be invested by spiritual heroes. She will be an easygoing woman who is meaningful to behold. Her area of activity will be in southern Tibet, on the Bhutanese border.

"An incarnation of your wisdom activities will be invested by enlightened body, speech, and mind. She will have a beautiful, appealing manner and possess the signs and marks of physical perfection. Any degree of connection with her will be meaningful. Her area of activity will be in northern Tibet, in a place called Khawa Tro.

"Tsogyal, create a catalog of the profound teachings and essential meditation instructions you've received. If you conceal them as Treasures and seal them with aspirations, these texts will be deeply helpful to others when your incarnations appear. I, Lotus-Born, will also reincarnate many times.

"The sharp quality of the teachings of the supreme approach of secret mantra will only last a short time. In general, you will be kind to the Tibetan people. However, those who lack fortune, who are ill-fated, or who foster corrupt or negative views will not understand your teachings.

"Without hypocrisy in relation to my doctrine, you cultivated your experience of every profound teaching. Therefore, once you cleanse this lifetime's residual obscurations, you will reach the spiritual attainment of uncontaminated life. You will then remain in this youthful body for sixty years, in the form of a reincarnate master in this realm. Then you will attain enlightenment in the expanse of uncontaminated great bliss."

This concludes the sixth chapter, in which I, the princess, receive prophecies.

Samaya
Gya Gya Gya

7: HOW THE PRINCESS SPREADS THE TEACHINGS FAR AND WIDE

Yeshé Tsogyal requested further guidance from Lotus-Born of Oddiyana.

"You kindly granted me these prophecies. Please give me the background instructions related to them. My incarnations and the teachings you've given me will appear together, at the same time. If I am to bring future beings to spiritual maturity and liberation as a teacher with these instructions, would it be suitable for me to catalog all the teachings and conceal them as profound Treasures? At the time when these meditation instructions will be most helpful, what sort of changes and problems will affect the doctrine? Which individuals will become the custodians for these teachings? In the end, how many beings will I place in states of lasting happiness? Please give me answers to these questions."

Lotus-Born of Oddiyana responded: "Dakini Yeshé Tsogyal, listen to me. Gather together the profound teachings I've given you, the account of your life that Bendé Sangyé Yeshé requested from you, the general prophecies related to the doctrine, the key to the Treasure proclamations, and these specific prophecies concerning individuals. List them in the catalog, place a doctrinal seal on each one, and conceal them with aspirations. This will prove to be an immense kindness for all future beings.

"At the time when these sacred teachings will bring beings to spiritual maturity, the Buddhist doctrine will be seriously diminished. As a result, the golden yoke of royal law will be broken, the silk knot of Buddhist law will be untied, the leather pouch of ministerial law will be ripped, and the woven rope of human society will be torn.

"The light of the Three Jewels' doctrine will fade, the stronghold of the listening attendants' law will be destroyed, the tree of training for awakened heroes will be uprooted, and the lake of secret mantra's tantric bonds will flood its banks.

"Children won't listen to their parents, subjects won't listen to their leaders, servants won't listen to their masters, women will be more highly regarded than men, Buddhist language will be used casually, the hungry will eat their promises, the thirsty will drink evil, and people will wear chain mail for clothing.

"The friends one relies on will be swindlers, people will commit great wrongdoing to gain wealth, heads of monasteries will become army generals, disciples will rise up as enemies, abbots will collect taxes, fully ordained monks and nuns will wield weapons, accomplished adepts will live in towns, charlatans will be very popular, practitioners will be taken by demons, good will be repaid with evil, the doctrine will be trivialized, all the statues will be turned upside down, and temples will be surrounded by military barricades.

"Siblings will lose their modesty, family conflicts will increase, lunatics and mad dogs will surface, epidemics will rage, frost and hail will spread like mist, bad omens and famine will be as thick as constellations, people won't think at all or will think too much, they will do nothing or do too much, and they will never suffer or suffer too much.

"A variety of unmanageable situations will arise. For the most part, beings will do only evil, allowing emanations of corrupt demons to overpower them. At that time, no one will have a sanctuary. Therefore, our incarnations, those of Tsogyal and Lotus-Born, will protect many individuals, bring them to spiritual maturity, and lead them to liberation.

"Specifically, here in the enclosure of the Tibetan Himalayas, there will be only five people who take to heart my profound doctrine and who will forge a meaningful connection with your life. One is the present-day Buddhist king Trisong Detsen. After many lifetimes, his final incarnation's area of activity will be in southern Tibet on the Bhutanese border. He will be known as Chökyi Wangchuk and greatly serve beings. That will be his last lifetime before attaining enlightenment.

"Another is the present-day mantra holder Chokdrup Tsal. After many lifetimes, his final incarnation's area of activity will be in a place called Dramo Yar. He will be known as Orgyen Lingpa and greatly serve beings. That will be his last lifetime before attaining complete enlightenment.

"Another is the present-day princess Pema Sal. After many lifetimes, her final incarnation's area of activity will be in Bumtang, Bhutan. She will be known as Drimé Öser and greatly serve beings. That will be her last lifetime before attaining complete enlightenment.

"Another is the present-day Lekjin Zangmo. After many lifetimes, her final incarnation's area of activity will be in a region called Tashi Zhong Lung. She will be known as Pema Benzra and greatly serve beings. That will be her last lifetime before attaining complete enlightenment.

"Another is the present-day Bendé Sangyé Yeshé. At death he will dissolve into my heart. Then, having already attained uncontaminated enlightenment, he will appear in the domain of the perception of devoted disciples in a place called Drada Kangmar. He will be known as Drimé Kunga or Drimé Kungé Nyingpo, and greatly serve beings. Tsogyal, he will especially take to heart all of your essential wisdom-mind teachings. Then he will place innumerable individuals, in the hundreds of thousands, at the level of spontaneous awareness holder."

Thus he spoke.

Lotus-Born of Oddiyana and Yeshé Tsogyal lived together inseparably for sixty years as they traveled in this realm, a pure land of enlightenment's form dimension of manifest embodiment. During that time, until Lotus-Born of Oddiyana left for the southwest, they appeared in whatever ways were needed to guide beings, and taught the unsurpassable doctrine.

Eventually, at dawn, on the tenth day of the Monkey month (the seventh lunar month) of the Monkey Year, he mounted a ray of light and left for Tail-Fan Island in the southwest.

As is well known, Supreme Lotus-Born of Oddiyana stayed for three thousand years in India and China and for one hundred eleven years in Tibet. Tsogyal was his close attendant from the time he arrived in Tibet, serving him until he left for the land to the southwest. When she was young, she subdued the demons that held corrupt views. During early adulthood, she settled in evenness within empty bliss. In the end, she attained enlightenment, indivisible with Dakini Lady Ever-Excellent.

This concludes the seventh chapter, which describes how I, the princess, will spread the spiritual teachings far and wide.

Samaya
Gya Gya Gya

Colophon

Amazing! This is my, Yeshé Tsogyal's, life story.
Unable to refuse the devoted request
of Bendé Sangyé Yeshé,
I composed this to serve the fortunate
and concealed it as a Treasure
for the welfare of future generations.

Keep it secret from unworthy recipients.
To alter it in any way
impairs your tantric bonds.
The four tribes of dakinis will be its able guardians
and will entrust it to a sublime individual at the right time.
Now I entrust it to you.

Samaya.
Seal of entrustment.
Seal of treasure.
Seal of concealment.
Khatam.

This Treasure was revealed by Drimé Kunga.

Index